THE PARKS
of
NEW MEXICO

A Traveler's Guide To
The Land of Enchantment
by
Nicky Leach

SIERRA PRESS
MARIPOSA, CA

DEDICATION

In memory of naturalist and early wilderness advocate Aldo Leopold, whose essay "Thinking Like a Mountain" in *A Sand County Almanac* first counted the human cost of losing wolves and wilderness in New Mexico; and to the diverse coalition of New Mexicans who have come together to fight for protection of Otero Mesa, Valle Vidal, Baca Ranch, and other unique wilderness areas in New Mexico.   —N.L.

ACKNOWLEDGMENTS

This book about the parks of my home state has a special place in my heart. I want to thank all those who offered generous editorial input during the research and writing, including: George Herring at Aztec National Monument; Joyce Umbach at Capulin Volcano National Monument; Paula Bauer and T.K. Kajiki at Carlsbad Caverns National Park; Ross Bodnar at Chaco Culture National Historical Park; Leslie de Long at El Malpais and El Morro National Monuments; Frank Torres at Fort Union National Monument; Sonya Berger at Gila Cliff Dwellings National Monument; Christine Beekman at Pecos National Historical Park; Diane Souder at Petroglyph National Monument; Norma Pineda at Salinas National Monument; John Mangimeli at White Sands National Monument; and Jere Krakow and Lee Kreutzer of the National Park Service, National Trails System - Salt Lake City. A special thank you to Chris Judson at Bandelier National Monument, who took time out from her schedule to review the entire text. Finally, I would like to thank two former neighbors and long-time friends, NPS historian Art Gomez and his wife Penny, for sharing their Southwest expertise (and very good margaritas) with me over the years.   —N.L.

INSIDE FRONT COVER
Soaptree yucca and the San Andres Mountains at sunset, White Sands National Monument.
PHOTO ©LARRY ULRICH

PAGE 2
Kiva and crumbled walls of Pueblo Bonito, Chaco Culture National Historical Park.
PHOTO ©SCOTT T. SMITH

TITLE PAGE
Cow skulls for sale in Rancho de Taos.
PHOTO ©CHUCK PLACE/Place Stock Photo

PAGE 4/5
Hoodoo at sunset, Bisti Badlands.
PHOTO ©TIM FITZHARRIS

CONTENTS

PAGE 6/7
Early morning at Gran Quivira, Salinas Pueblo Missions
National Monument. PHOTO ©WILLARD CLAY
PAGE 7 (BELOW)
Fajada Butte and rising moon at sunset, Chaco Culture
National Historical Park. PHOTO ©JON MARK STEWART

The Land of Enchantment

Kivas at Pueblo Bonito, Chaco Culture National Historical Park. PHOTO ©ED CALLAERT

It's a hot early fall day in northern New Mexico. I'm here on an overnight trip to Chaco Culture National Historical Park, the Vatican City of the early Pueblo world. My companions and I have climbed the narrow slot trail that leads to the clifftop and now stand directly above Chaco's most famous ruin: Pueblo Bonito. The D-shaped great house, with its 650 rooms and 30 kivas, is impressive enough at ground level; up here, though, it's obvious that Chaco's architects designed it to be first seen from above, where the extensive road system enters the canyon via Pueblo Alto.

It takes a leap of imagination to cross centuries and place ourselves inside the minds of Chaco's leaders. The buildings they erected were designed to last. The entire Chaco environment, suggests Chaco archaeologist Stephen Lekson, is a "ritual landscape," where the man-made environment speaks directly to the natural world. Public structures, architectural features, and roads—with alignments to cardinal directions; the moon, stars, and planets; as well as mountains, cliffs, buttes, and other natural features—reflect a uniquely Chacoan, highly ordered way of viewing the universe. It's one where even the smallest details, such as ineffably beautiful mosaic-like walls hidden beneath thick plaster, still move us in a way we struggle to comprehend.

It was all nearly lost. In the late 1800s, Chaco and other important Pueblo ruins in New Mexico, Colorado, Utah, and Arizona were system-atically robbed of their precolumbian treasures by tourists, settlers, even foreign archaeologists. New Mexico's first ethnologist, Adolph Bandelier, sounded the alarm in his 1890 report. Then three world's expositions alerted Americans to the antiquities being lost from Southwest pueblos. In 1900, the *Santa Fe New Mexican* newspaper weighed in, denouncing Colorado cowboy Richard "Anasazi" Wetherill, who had excavated Mesa Verde, for removing Chaco's ancient artifacts and building a homestead among the ruins.

Key to the debate was archaeologist Edgar Lee Hewett, who excavated Bandelier National Monument and Chaco Canyon in the early 1900s. A persuasive, thoughtful educator with Midwest farming roots and eastern connections, Hewett drafted the version of the Antiquities Act passed by Congress in 1906, using his bully pulpit as first director of the western branch of the Archaeological Institute of America in Santa Fe. Four-hundred-year-old Santa Fe, it turned out, was the right place at the right time, and Hewett the right man, to make a lasting contribution to American history.

In subsequent decades, national monuments were set aside in New Mexico by the U.S. president or Congress to preserve their unique human and scientific values. The first, in 1906, was El Morro, a bluff in northwestern New Mexico bearing the inscriptions of important historical figures. Chaco Canyon came next, in 1907; it was upgraded to Chaco Culture National Historical Park in 1980, after its extensive road system and outlying pueblos were found. Also designated in 1907 was Gila Cliff Dwellings in southwestern New Mexico, a unique Mogollon cliff pueblo.

The spectacular cave dwellings and pueblos in the Jemez Mountains received protection as Bandelier National Monument in 1916, the same year Capulin Volcano in northeastern New Mexico became a national monument. In 1923, Aztec Pueblo, a Chacoan outlier in north-western New Mexico, was preserved, along with Carlsbad Cave National Monument (it was redesignated Carlsbad Caverns National Park in 1930). The extraordinary gypsum dunes at White Sands received national monument status in 1933. Fort Union, one of the largest 19th-century supply forts in the Southwest, was set aside in 1956.

Not until 1965 were the pueblo and Spanish mission at Pecos, east of Santa Fe, given protection. The important Civil War battlefield at Glorieta Pass was added when the park was expanded and redesignated a national historical park in 1990; other important sites at the park were added the following year. In 1980, three national monuments were set aside in New Mexico: the Spanish pueblo missions of Gran Quivira, Quarai, and Abo known as Salinas Pueblo Missions National Monument; Petroglyph National Monument, a lava escarpment in western Albuquer-que bearing 20,000 Indian, Spanish, and Anglo inscriptions; and El Malpais, which with the adjoining BLM-managed conservation area, protects volcanic features associated with Mount Taylor in northwestern New Mexico. Kasha-Katuwe Tent Rocks National Monument was designated in 2000 to protect eroded volcanic rocks on Cochiti Pueblo land. One of a new breed of minimally developed landscape monuments, it is managed by the BLM.

New Mexico played a vital role in this country's early preserva-tion history, but as the Antiquities Act turns 100 in 2006, the state's quieter,

Winter morning at White Sands National Monument.

less-visited national parks and monuments tend to be overshadowed by headliners in adjoining states, such as Mesa Verde in Colorado, the Grand Canyon in Arizona, and Utah's Arches, Canyonlands, and Zion national parks. New Mexico's principal draws today are historic Santa Fe, Taos, and Albuquerque, Hispanic and Indian arts and crafts, and Indian pueblos whose year round dances harken back to ancient times. Fewer people leave enough time to make day trips to national parks within striking distance of Santa Fe, Albuquerque, and Taos and southern New Mexico cities like Carlsbad, Las Cruces, and Silver City.

I wrote this book because, for 18 years, I have specialized in introducing people to New Mexico's national parks and monuments. Where else can you see so many ancient Pueblo ruins once occupied by ancestors of people living in New Mexico's 19 contemporary pueblos? Meet Hispanic New Mexicans whose ancestors arrived with Coronado 400 years ago? Or view thousand-year-old symbols carved in the rock that are still used in ceremonies today? In New Mexico, history leaps off the page and becomes a literal touchstone to the past. All you have to do is reach out. *Bienvenidos*—welcome—to the Land of Enchantment.

The energetic dancing of the Tewa Ceremonial Dancers, Nambe Pueblo.

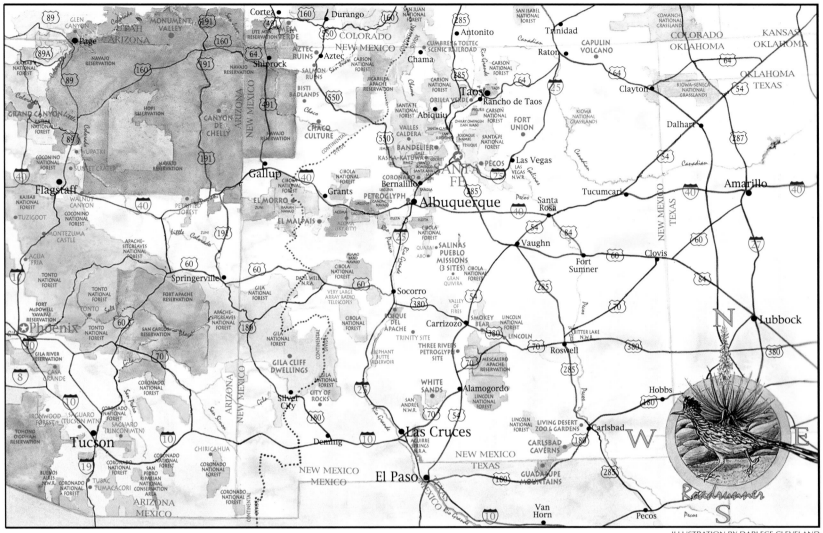

ILLUSTRATION BY DARLECE CLEVELAND

New Mexico is 122,666 square miles in size and is centrally located on the southwestern U.S.–Mexico border. It overlaps the Chihuahuan and Sonoran deserts, the Great Plains, the Southern Rocky Mountains, and the Colorado Plateau. The state contains 13 national parks and monuments, 20 percent of which are dedicated to geological features.

Near Raton in northeastern New Mexico, Capulin Volcano National Monument is south of Interstate 25, along US 64/87, a major travel link between New Mexico and Texas. Northwest of Santa Fe, on NM 4 in the Jemez Mountains, are Bandelier National Monument and Valles Caldera National Preserve, connected to the world's largest caldera. West of Albuquerque, off Interstate 40, are Petroglyph and El Malpais national monuments, with their youthful volcanoes and lava flows. El Malpais is located on NM 53, just east of El Morro National Monument, an eroded sandstone headland that preserves historic inscriptions.

Carlsbad Caverns National Park, beneath the Guadalupe Mountains of southeastern New Mexico off US 62/180, preserves extraordinary cave formations located in one of only two accessible underground Permian Reefs in the world. White Sands National Monument, located in the neighboring Tularosa Basin off US 70/82, has silver dunes made of wind-blown gypsum that washed out of highlands.

Gila Cliff Dwellings National Monument is at the end of 44-mile-long NM 15, north of Silver City, reached via US 180. Its location, above a tributary of the Gila River, is what attracted its builders during drought conditions. Chaco Culture National Historical Park and Aztec Ruins National Monument are both located off US 550, the main highway to the Four Corners in northwestern New Mexico. Chaco's location in the remote San Juan Basin made it vulnerable during extended drought but Salmon and Aztec were built on San Juan River

tributaries, allowing them to thrive much longer.

Pecos National Historical Park, 20 miles east of Santa Fe, off Interstate 25 was once on an important mountain pass south of the Sangre de Cristo Mountains with few natural resources. The same is true of Gran Quivira, Abo, and Quarai— the three Salinas Pueblo Missions surrounding Mountainair in the Estancia Basin, south of Interstate 40, east of Albuquerque. All of the modern New Mexico pueblos, except Picuris, Zuni, Acoma, and Laguna, are located close to the Rio Grande, which bissects the state north to south, from Colorado to Mexico. The Jicarilla Apache Reservation is located between US 550 and US 64 in northeastern New Mexico. The Mescalero Apache Reservation is near Ruidoso, off US 70/380, in southeastern New Mexico. The Navajo Nation spans northwestern New Mexico, northeastern Arizona and southern Utah and can be accessed in New Mexico via US 550 and US 64, and by US 160 and US 191 in Arizona.

PAGE 12/13: Sandhill cranes and snow geese at Bosque del Apache National Wildlife Refuge, sunset. PHOTO ©TIM FITZHARRIS

THE GEOLOGY OF NEW MEXICO

Mudcracks and playa at sunset, Animas Valley. PHOTO ©ROBERT HILDEBRAND

For most of New Mexico's history, it lay underwater. Throughout the Precambrian and Paleozoic eras—when North America was part of a vast supercontinent dubbed Pangaea that was tilted down on its western edge, allowing the sea to encroach—the state languished in a submarine environment, building itself up, layer by sedimentary layer, on the seafloor. Deposits from early calcareous algae and other marine lifeforms mingled with coastal sands, settled, compressed, and hardened into limestone, sandstone, and shale cemented by calcium, manganese, and iron.

Movements along faults allowed heat to escape from the earth's mantle. Molten rock, or magma, was injected into sedimentary rocks, uplifting and folding them into tall mountain chains with a core of hard metamorphic gneiss, schist, and igneous granite. Wind and water attacked these highlands, wearing them down into sediments again. Over and over, they redeposited, hardened, uplifted, and folded. Today, these 1.3-million-year-old Precambrian rocks are all but invisible, evident only in the Sangre de Cristo Mountains and near Tres Piedras, north of Ojo Caliente.

In southern New Mexico, 250 million years ago, the sea was trapped in a series of large bays that often dried out before flooding again. One large embayment, in the Permian Basin, was filled with sponges, trilobites, nautiloids, ammonites, brachiopods, and a type of foraminifera called fusilinids, which formed a 400-mile-long Permian-era barrier reef. Most of this marine life suffered a mass extinction when the climate warmed and the sea withdrew to the west. Evaporites, such as salt, potash, and gypsum, entombed the reef for more than 150 million years.

The ecological niche left empty by the Permian extinction was quickly occupied by dinosaurs during the warm, tropical Triassic and Jurassic periods of the Mesozoic Era, 250 to 200 million years ago. One of the earth's first dinosaurs, the meat-eating Coelophysis, was discovered in large numbers in the brightly colored sedimentary Triassic rocks surrounding Ghost Ranch. Paleontologists have also found the bones of Stegosaurus, Allosaurus, and Camarasaurus, dated to the Jurassic Period, in the state. A rare late Cretaceous Period dinosaur fossil, *Alamoaurus Sanjuanensis*, America's last sauropod, was uncovered in the Bisti Badlands and De-na-zin Wilderness, south of Farmington, where erosion has carved eerie badlands in what was once an ancient sea coast.

The Sahara-like desert that formed in the Jurassic period during a warming, drying trend blew sand into towering sand dunes across much of the West. These dunes solidified into sandstone known variously in New Mexico as the Wingate, Navajo, Entrada, Zuni, and Gallup Sandstone. The petrified dunes were later covered by succeeding marine and shoreline sediments, which cemented and hardened the sandstone and tinted it with iron into the glorious hues of vermilion, salmon, rose, and orange so beautifully displayed throughout the Canyon Country of the Colorado Plateau.

For the dinosaurs, and many other living things, the finale was brief and deadly. Apparently as a result of an asteroid colliding with the earth in the Gulf of Mexico at the end of the Cretaceous Period, 65 million year ago, the dinosaurs were wiped out, paving the way for flowers and mammals, and eventually humans, to take center stage.

Pangaea broke apart into continental plates that drifted on the convection currents created by the earth's outer layer, or mantle, a part of the earth that is solid but plastic allowing slow, flowing movement. The North American Plate collided with the Farallon Plate, the eastern edge of the Pacific Oceanic Crust off present-day California, forcing the Farallon Plate under the North American Plate. The reverberations sent seismic shock waves eastward through the deep-seated Precambrian faults in the bedrock. The Rocky Mountains, and their southern extension, the Sangre de Cristo Mountains of New Mexico, and the Colorado Plateau began to rise.

Movement along local faults on the Colorado Plateau during the Oligocene Epoch, 30 million years ago, caused other significant landforms to appear. The Rio Grande Rift in central New Mexico began to pull apart the land in between. One of the major rift valleys in the world, it continues to widen and may eventually form an interior seaway, not unlike the one that once covered New Mexico. West of the San Juan Basin, high plateaus formed, incorporating the eastern edge of the Colorado Plateau and the volcanic Datil-Mogollon Highlands in western New Mexico.

In southern New Mexico, fault blocks moved up sharply in relation to each other, creating small, craggy ranges and accompanying basins. What is now the Tularosa Basin appeared when a dome formation,

Formations at Kasha–Katuwe Tent Rocks National Monument. PHOTO ©MARY LIZ AUSTIN

Papoose Room, Carlsbad Caverns. PHOTO ©STEVE MULLIGAN

known as an anticline, collapsed, leaving behind the San Andres and Sacramento mountains. The basin eventually filled with gypsum, washed down from the highlands and blown on southeasterly winds into large sculpted dunes at White Sands National Monument.

In the neighboring Permian Basin, around 17 million years ago, uplift of the Guadalupe Mountains caused water from the surface to circulate through cracks and faults in the limestone of the Guadalupe Mountains. When this water encountered hydrogen-sulfide-rich brines formed from nearby oil and gas deposits, sulfuric acid was created. This powerful acid sculpted the large cave passages far below the water table. Carlsbad Cavern was formed in this way between three and five million years ago, but other caves in the Guadalupe Mountains are as much as 11 million years old.

As uplift continued, the large cave passages drained. Water from rain and snow continued to seep into the rock. This water, enriched with carbon-dioxide from the atmosphere and soil, formed a weak acid that dissolved small amounts of the limestone. When this water reached the cave and lost carbon-dioxide, it left behind tiny crystals of the dissolved calcium carbonate. Over hundreds of thousands of years, this process created the thousands of stalactites, stalagmites, soda straws, helictites, lily pads, cave pearls, and other speleotherms seen in the caves today.

While much of Carlsbad Cavern has been inactive since the end of the last ice age 10,000 years ago, there are places in Carlsbad Cavern and other caves in the Guadalupe Mountains where speleotherms are still forming.

The Jemez Mountains, west of the Rio Grande on an active fault geologists call the Jemez Lineament, began forming 15 million years ago. Valles Caldera appeared 1.2 million years ago, the collapsed center of the central Jemez volcanic field. From the east, the drive to Valle Grande—an area between resurgent domes that formed inside the Valles Caldera after the center collapsed—crosses the Pajarito Plateau. This plateau is made of welded ash, or tuff, which was excavated by Pueblo people for homes in what is now Bandelier National Monument. Tuff from another volcano created the strangely eroded pinnacles of Kasha-Katuwe Tent Rocks National Monument on the nearby Cochiti Indian Reservation. From the top of lovely Capulin Volcano, in northeastern New Mexico, you can see

8,818-foot-high Sierra Grande, a Hawaiian-style andesitic volcano formed by successive eruptions beginning 4 million years ago, Capulin itself is a young volcano, built about 62,000 years ago.

Most dramatic of all may be the numerous volcanic necks and dikes and lava flows revealed by erosion, which form a striking contrast with pale sedimentary rocks. The 650-foot-deep chasm carved by the Rio Grande through lava flows west of Taos is part of a huge plateau visible for miles. Valley of Fires Recreation Area, in south-central New Mexico, preserves the Carrizozo Flow, and rivals El Malpais National Monument for having the youngest lava flow in the state. The nearby Puerco Valley in northwestern New Mexico, home to part of the Navajo Reservation, has more volcanic necks than anywhere else in the world, including Cabezon Peak, a major landmark on the reservation.

To almost all of these rocks are attached stories, a human way of making friends with the lithic world. Places like Three Rivers Petroglyphs and Petroglyph National Monument preserve thousands of important symbols and rock writings made by generations of Indian, Spanish, and Anglo people. Those on the sandstone bluff at El Morro National Monument, dubbed Inscription Rock, form a sweeping record of centuries of New Mexico history. They were thought so important they were preserved as New Mexico's first national monument in 1906.

Within the past three million years, rivers entering the Rio Grande Rift, and the Rio Grande itself, cut down into a series of linked basins in the central part of the state, shaping canyons and leaving behind more than a mile of sediments. These hardened into the loose, colorful conglomerate of the Santa Fe Group, which has eroded into mesas, buttes, and hills, often preserved by caprocks of lava less than a few thousand years old. Along NM 14 (popularly known as the Turquoise Trail), the Cerrillos Hills and Ortiz Mountains yielded large quantities of turquoise mined by Ancestral Pueblo people and traded as far as Mexico a thousand years ago. In the 1500s, Spanish colonists mined lead and silver in this region, while 19th-century Anglo settlers briefly extracted gold from the Ortiz Mountains. Copper continues to be mined in large quantities at the massive Santa Rita Mine near Silver City, which, as it name implies, grew up around a very different precious metal.

OPPOSITE: Boulders at sunset, City of Rocks State Park. PHOTO ©LAURENCE PARENT

FLORA AND FAUNA

New Mexico's state bird: the roadrunner PHOTO ©TIM FITZHARRIS

New Mexico ranks fourth in the nation for biodiversity. Altogether the state is home to 154 species of mammals, 98 reptile and 26 amphibian species, 120 fish species, 447 species of birds, and 3,305 plant species. A total of 90 species are endemic. At 3,000–5,000 feet, southern New Mexico's Chihuahuan Desert is in the Lower Sonoran Life Zone, with chilly winters and occasional snowfalls and summers exceeding 100 degrees Fahrenheit. Desert shrubs shed their leaves or shut down during hot, dry periods; others close up or tilt fleshy, waxy leaves away from direct sunlight to keep cool. Cacti have done away with leaves altogether. They have spines for protection but photosynthesize food along their large stems or pads. In spring, cacti sport showy flowers with large pollen centers to attract pollinators. At night, bats and moths visit creamy, luminous blossoms while, in daylight, birds and butterflies are attracted by red and yellow blossoms.

Native people had uses for many of these tough desert plants. By early fall, pricklypear cactus are covered in juicy edible red fruits beloved by animals and humans. Native people have used the roots of the yucca, the state plant (and actually in the lily family), for shampoo, the fibers for clothing, and the fruit as starchy food for centuries. The Mescalero Apache roasted agave hearts in ceremonies. Ancient roasting pits can be seen at Carlsbad Caverns. Agaves, also, are in the lily family.

Desert animals usually hunt at night and stay cool in burrows and dens or under rocks in the daytime. Coyotes become active at dusk and dawn, traveling between sheltered canyons and desert hunting grounds in search of cottontails, jackrabbits, and kangaroo rats, which recycle all the water they need from seeds. In McKittrick Canyon in the Guadalupe Mountains, dense stands of Texas madrone trees turn red in fall. Mountain lion live here, attracted by a sizeable mule deer population.

Arizona cypress and plate-barked alligator juniper mingle with Chihuahua and Apache pine on the U.S.–Mexico border. "Sky Islands" created by basin-and-range faulting support forests of Douglas fir, aspen, and ponderosa pine. They provide browse for white-tailed deer and shelter sulphur-bellied flycatchers, Mexican chickadees, and the elegant trogon, a Sierra Madre native that breeds in the Chiricahua Mountains each May. Most visible are hummingbirds. A record number of species return seasonally to the Gila National Forest, north of Silver City, where they cluster around feeders. The extreme southwest of New Mexico, the "bootheel," is prime habitat for collared lizards and poisonous Gila monsters. The roadrunner, New Mexico's state bird and a member of the cuckoo family, is a key inhabitant of this area. Desert bighorn sheep thrive in the hot, rugged hills near Lordsburg and use the lower Gila River.

The alkali flats, or *playas*, of southeastern New Mexico are harsh territory but saltbush, iodinebush, pickleweed, and other salt-tolerant species manage to live here. At White Sands National Monument, soaptree yucca stays one step ahead of shifting dunes by growing fast enough to avoid burial. Fringe-toed lizards and two species of rattlesnake—the western diamondback and desert massassauga—inhabit the dunes. White camouflage allows more common animals, such as rabbits, to blend in and hide from predators. Animals living amid lava flows have dark coats while those living below-ground have become blind in the darkness, a feature of cave creatures such as eyeless beetles and crickets found in Carlsbad's limestone caverns. Carlsbad is most famous for its 300,000 Brazilian (commonly called Mexican) free-tailed bats, which live in one of the cave rooms near the Natural Entrance.

In the widespread Upper Sonoran Life Zone (4,000–7,000 feet), the principal species are dwarf pinyon and juniper trees; scrub oak; native grasses such as ricegrass and blue grama; pricklypear and cholla cactus. Fragrant pinyons, prized for their nuts, and shaggy-barked juniper cloak the foothills of northern New Mexico. Overgrazing and a devastating bark-beetle invasion sparked by drought have doomed many pinyons. Sagebrush and rabbitbrush, known as *chamisa*, are taking over.

In northeastern New Mexico, the Rockies open out to grassy plains, home to free-ranging pronghorn, reintroduced managed herds of bison, and hundreds of bird species, including the flamboyant lesser prairie chicken. Here too are endangered black-tailed prairie dogs, the principal prey of black-footed ferrets, one of the most endangered animals in the world. Capulin Volcano has a surprising annual wildlife event: swarms of ladybugs rest on the forested rim each summer.

Above 7,000 feet, Transition Zone forests include Gambel oak and ponderosa pine, a tall airy beauty that grows in the Jemez, Sangre de Cristo, Sacramento, and Mogollon mountains. Abert's squirrels, Steller's jays, mule deer, and black bear live here, along with ubiquitous ravens

Claret-cup cactus in Chaco Canyon. PHOTO ©LARRY ULRICH

Black-tailed jackrabbit. PHOTO ©TIM FITZHARRIS

Black-tailed prairie dogs. PHOTO ©TIM FITZHARRIS

whose hoarse croaks are common throughout the desert. Wildflowers bloom in waves, and include Rocky Mountain penstemon, Indian paintbrush, lupine, verbena, skyrock gilia, milkvetch, and purple aster, sunflowers, and other composites.

Douglas fir, spruce, and aspen dominate the Mixed Conifer Zone, above 8,500 feet. Mule deer and Rocky Mountain elk are popular game species in the forests, which also support yellow-bellied marmots, pika, blue grouse, and birds such as Clark's nutcracker and hermit thrush. Above 9,500 feet, Englemann spruce, subalpine fir, corkbark fir, bristlecone pine, and other cool-weather conifers occupy the Subalpine Zone. Plants mat close together on the ground, conserve moisture with woody stems, and have small flowers. Hawks and eagles migrate over the central Sandia and Manzano Mountains in fall.

Eighty percent of wildlife relies on rivers, streams, *bosque* bottomlands, lakes, and *cienega* marshes. The dammed Rio Grande has lost many native cottonwood and willow *bosque* bottomlands. They are preserved in Albuquerque's Rio Grande Nature Center, where you'll find Cooper's hawks, Canada geese, black-capped chickadees, turtles, and toads, along with beaver whose dams create shady resting areas for fish, insects, and other animals. Bosque del Apache, south of Socorro, is one of New Mexico's five spectacular national wildlife refuges. Thousands of sandhill cranes overwinter here along with snow geese, kestrels, northern harriers, golden eagles, and other birds. The dawn takeoff of thousands of birds from the refuge is one of the great wildlife sights in the world.

Sandhill cranes preparing to land, Bosque del Apache. PHOTO ©STEVE TRAUDT

THE PREHISTORIC WORLD

Pueblo Bonito, Chaco Culture National Historical Park. PHOTO ©ED CALLAERT

In 1926, archaeologist Jesse Figgins excavated two fluted stone spearpoints and a third buried in the ribs of a giant extinct bison in an arroyo near Folsom in northeastern New Mexico. First discovered in 1908 by self-educated black cowboy George McJunkin, the Folsom Site proved beyond a doubt that big-game hunters were in New Mexico at the end of the Ice Age, 10,000 years ago. Seven years later, when archaeologist Edgar Howard excavated a gravel pit in Blackwater Draw, near the town of Clovis, he found not only Folsom-era spearpoints and bison bones but also differently knapped Clovis spearpoints and mammoth bones that predated those of Folsom Man by 2,000 years. They were dubbed the Clovis and are the oldest known inhabitants of New Mexico.

Other sites yielded 8,000-year-old spearpoints, the Eden Point, designed by later Cody-era hunters to bring down buffalo, a descendant of the giant bison. When the climate changed again, in 5,000 B.C., the buffalo migrated to the cooler, northern plains, and with them went the paleo-hunters.

The warmer, drier temperatures allowed new species of edible roots, shoots, fruits, seeds, and nuts to grow in the Southwest. Hunter-gatherers of the Archaic culture became skilled harvesters of wild foods. They moved with the seasons, using baskets to collect plants as they ripened, and hunted deer, bighorn sheep, elk, and other game in the mountains in fall and winter. By 1,000 B.C., the population of New Mexico had grown to 15,000–30,000 people living in clan-based villages of semi-subterranean, oval pithouses with roofs of logs and earth.

The Cochise people, who lived in southern New Mexico, were the first to experiment with farming in 2,000 B.C., after obtaining corn—domesticated from a wild grass called *teosinte*—through neighbors in Mexico. By A.D. 400, Cochise descendants, the Mogollon, were not only growing corn and squash but a precursor of the pinto bean, which improved health by providing necessary amino acids in the diet. The Western Mogollon lived west of the Rio Grande and the Jornada Mogollon lived to the east, in the Tularosa Basin, in pithouse villages with community centers—the Southwest's first *pueblos*.

Mogollon people also learned how to make pottery, another important Mexican innovation, favored over baskets for storage, transportation, and cooking. Early Mogollon pottery was a simple brownware

coiled into basket shapes, later refined into a beautiful redware. Between A.D. 1000 and 1150, the Mimbres branch mingled with Ancestral Pueblo people to the north and started making black-on-white ceramics. Mimbres pottery was prized for its superb quality, unusual animal motifs, and fascinating depictions of daily life as part of a huge trade network that included the powerful centers of Chaco Canyon to the north and Casas Grandes (Paquime) in Chihuahua to the south. The Mogollon eventually seem to have moved in with Ancestral Pueblo people to the north across the area now known as the Mogollon Rim, where their rectangular kivas survive.

A warming trend in the 700s may have led people to congregate in the first above-ground stone villages, or *pueblos*. Structures made of woven mud and sticks (*jacal*) laid out in arcs, two rooms deep, were probably used for storage at first and then became residences. Later buildings were constructed of shaped stones, mortared with mud, and covered with plaster.

Pueblo construction reached its most beautiful aesthetic expression in villages and preplanned ceremonial centers constructed by people of the Chaco culture. At least 10,000 farming hamlets were founded in the Chaco region during the Pueblo II period (A.D. 850–1000), despite climatic uncertainty. The location of Chaco Canyon, in the center of the San Juan Basin at the boundary of two distinct seasonal rainfall patterns, may have helped it grow into an important redistribution and ceremonial center. Some 100 overscaled public buildings with storage facilities and room suites, known as great houses, and huge circular underground ceremonial chambers, or great kivas, were linked to farming hamlets by roads radiating from Chaco Canyon across a 40,000-square-mile area. These massive buildings had 30-feet-high, tapering walls stabilized with core-and-veneer construction and dry-laid with such extraordinary precision and finesse they survive today.

Archaeologists have found that Chaco's leaders were not just clever entrepreneurs overseeing a far-flung, pre-European contact corporate empire but skilled astronomers who tracked planetary movements and organized whole landscapes—manmade and natural—into interdependent units geared toward maximization of resources. A period of greater rainfall may have consolidated their power, but when long

Doorways at Aztec Ruins National Monument. PHOTO ©TOM TILL

Cliff detail at Long House, Bandelier National Monument. PHOTO ©STEVE MULLIGAN

droughts ensued, the Chaco Phenomenon, as it is known, started to collapse.

The leaders at first seem to have responded by ordering the construction of more great houses, perhaps for storage and to bolster morale. Between 1088 and 1090, Salmon Pueblo was built near the San Juan River, followed in 1115 by nearby Aztec Pueblo on the Animas River, which Chaco Project archaeologist Stephen Lekson theorizes may have been intended as a new Chaco center. But by 1140, Chaco's great houses were all vacant, their inhabitants scattered. During the Pueblo IV period (A.D. 1150–1300), architectural evidence indicates that people from the Mesa Verde area in Colorado may have moved into former Chacoan strongholds, remodeled buildings, and made a different type of black-on-white pottery.

Although they are an anomaly, the most famous pueblo sites today are the villages built during the 1200s high up in the cliffs. These cliff dwellings were usually located in canyons, above reliable water sources and below mesa-top fields. Their location may indicate the need to defend villages and scarce resources from outsiders. Cliff dwellings were built by cultures as diverse as Mesa Verde and Kayenta Pueblo and Sinagua, Salado, and Mogollon.

Families began systematically leaving the drought-ridden Four Corners in the 1100s. Some clans walked to Arizona's Hopi Mesas. Others headed to the Jemez Mountains, where they dug out cave homes in the volcanic cliffs and built small pueblos on the Pajarito Plateau at what is now Bandelier National Monument. Their departure may have been hastened by the arrival of nomadic Athabascans from northwestern Canada who split culturally into the Navajo and Apache in the Southwest. The Apache held fiercely to their hunter-gatherer roots in the mountains, but the Navajo stayed in northern New Mexico and became herders and farmers, learning corn cultivation, weaving, and other skills from Pueblo neighbors. According to their own oral histories and new scientific evidence, Navajos may have been living in the Farmington area as early as 1175, increasing pressure on marginal lands.

A cooling trend in the 1300s and a huge influx of newcomers led many clans in the Rio Grande area to move down to the Rio Grande, where they built large pueblos of up to 1,000 rooms some 2–3 miles apart.

When conquistador Francisco Vasquez de Coronado made the first official Spanish *Entrada* into New Mexico in 1540, searching for gold, he found some 150 pueblos at Zuni, Hopi, and the Rio Grande area, with a total of up to 130,000 people. Nearby were remnants of large abandoned pueblos, such as Arroyo Hondo, southeast of Santa Fe in the Galisteo Basin, whose residents had starved following a long drought. Surviving pueblos were smaller than their predecessors and built closer together to discourage raids by Apaches, Navajos, and other newcomers. They occupied large tracts of land between the rivers and the mountains, where they farmed; hunted; mined turquoise, obsidian, and other precious stones; and made treks to collect salt from the dry lakebed in the Estancia Basin.

Pueblos such as Pecos, near Santa Fe, and Pueblo de las Humanas, the Gran Quivira unit of what is now Salinas Pueblo Missions National Historical Park in central New Mexico, were major trade centers on a cultural frontier, occupied by a changing cosmopolitan population of Pueblos and visiting Comanche, Ute, and Apache traders, who bartered buffalo hides for pottery, corn, jewelry, and cotton. These trading pueblos would play a pivotal role in the coming years, as ambitious Spanish colonists arrived, once again shaking the foundations of the Indian world.

THE MODERN WORLD

Eighteenth-century Morada de la Conquistadora Chapel, El Rancho de las Golondrinas, Santa Fe. PHOTO ©LAURENCE PARENT

In 1536, survivors of an ill-fated Spanish expedition to Florida straggled into Mexico City, capital of New Spain, after an eight-year trek from the Texas coast, telling stories of great cities to the north bursting with treasure. Two years later, Fray Marcos de Niza and one of the survivors, a Moor named Esteban, were sent to verify these accounts. Fray Marcos returned to Mexico after Esteban was slain in Cibola, the Spanish name for seven of the Indian pueblos of Zuni. Based on the priest's favorable reports, Francisco Vasquez de Coronado, accompanied by 336 soldiers, 1,000 Indians, four priests, four Spanish wives, and numerous wives and children of Indians, set out on February 1540 from Compostela, hoping to find a "New" Mexico as rich as the old.

New Mexico's wealth lay in the land itself and its industrious people, and Coronado returned to Mexico the following year empty-handed. In 1598, Don Juan de Oñate was named first governor of New Mexico and traveled to *El Norte* to exploit its natural resources and convert its Indians to Christianity. The colonists chose Ohkay Owingeh (San Juan Pueblo), near Española, as the site of the first capital. Some months later, the settlement was shifted to Yunque, on the west bank of the river, and renamed San Gabriel.

Oñate was relieved of his command due to his harsh treatment of both colonists and Pueblos. On one infamous occasion, he sentenced 20 young Acoma Pueblo men to have their right foot amputated following the killing of 13 Spaniards, including his nephew. Don Pedro de Peralta, his successor, moved the capital to a tributary of the Rio Grande by 1610, laying out Santa Fe atop the ruined pueblo of Ogapoge. The Palace of the Governors, on the north side of the Plaza, was built as administrative headquarters.

Missionaries targeted pueblos for missions. A priest would petition the *cacique* (religious leader of the pueblo) for entry and receive a building for use as a residence and church. Neophytes then assisted the priest in building a large, elaborate church with adjoining *convento*, or residence, pastures, and fields. The fathers introduced fruit and wheat farming, breadmaking in a Moorish-style outdoor beehive oven known as an *horno*, silversmithing, and cattle for meat, tallow for candles and soap, tanned cowhide, glue, and other products introduced from Europe.

Favored colonists and priests each required the pueblos to pay tribute, or *encomienda*, annually, in the form of bushels of corn and pieces of woven cotton cloth, or *mantas*. The Pueblos exhausted themselves working for their rulers and growing enough corn and cotton for themselves and Indian trading partners. In 1680, led by Popé, an elder from Ohkay Owingeh, the Pueblos rose up against their oppressors, killing the Spanish priests and expelling Spanish settlers south to El Paso, Texas.

After an initial struggle Don Diego de Vargas reconquered New Mexico in 1692, and the Pueblos reluctantly ceded to Spanish rule. In return, the Spaniards abolished *encomienda* and adopted a policy of tolerance toward Indian religion. Spanish law now acknowledged sovereignty of each pueblo—still recognized today—and the rights of residents to carry out their own religious observances.

During the 1700s, pueblo people taught Spaniards settling in remote areas how to build *placitas*, or family compounds, of thick-walled, mud-plastered homes with enclosed *portals* (porches), flat roofs, gypsum-washed mud plaster, and packed dirt floors cured with blood. Pueblos learned how to build with adobe by pouring mud strengthened by straw and hair into forms to make bricks that were sundried and made into high walls. Together, Pueblos and Spaniards fought a mutual enemy: marauding Apaches, Navajos, Utes, and Comanches moving south into New Mexico after being pushed off their lands by American settlers moving west.

Within months of Mexico winning independence from Spain in 1821, American traders began arriving in Santa Fe from Missouri along the 900-mile Santa Fe Trail. By 1846, relations between the United States and Mexico had deteriorated into war. In June, the state capital was peacefully occupied by the U.S. Army of the West under Gen. Stephen Kearny, and, in 1848, Mexico formally ceded the Southwest to the United States. The U.S. Army was based at Fort Marcy, in Santa Fe, and Fort Union, in northeastern New Mexico, where soldiers protected travelers on the Santa Fe Trail.

French-born Bishop Jean-Baptiste Lamy was named head of the Catholic Church in New Mexico. He swiftly imposed mainstream church authority over the homegrown Penitente religion of the Mexican period by building European-style churches and the first schools and colleges in Santa Fe. The Penitentes had taken hold in villages as a self-help system

Interior of San Miguel Mission, Santa Fe. PHOTO ©BRUCE HUCKO

Cathedral Basilica of St. Francis of Assisi, Santa Fe. PHOTO ©CHUCK PLACE/Place Stock Photo

after the Spanish government had withdrawn its priests at the end of Spanish rule in 1821. In Penitente villages, such as Abiquiu, the priests, or *hermanos,* were forced to toe the line or be excommunicated—an action that drove the folk religion underground, where it remains today, shrouded in secrecy.

A year after taking office, the first American governor, Charles Bent, a former mountain man and colleague of Kit Carson, was murdered in his Taos home. By the time the last two territorial governors, Lew Wallace and Bradford Prince, occupied the by-now decrepit, much-remodeled Palace of the Governors, at the end of the 1800s, it was viewed as an embarassing anachronism, synonymous with an Indian and Hispanic past that held back statehood.

New Mexico's antiquities captured the attention of archaeologists and anthropologists like Adolph Bandelier and Edgar Lee Hewett, who visited and excavated pueblos under the aegis of the American Institute of Archaeology. The arrival of the railroad in 1880 attracted entrepreneurs like Fred Harvey, who saw tourism potential in the West's scenic and archaeological treasures. As World War I loomed, wealthy Americans stopped vacationing in Europe and rediscovered America, helped by modern transportation, tourist guides, and a fascination with Indian cultures thought to be dying out.

Hewett followed up Bandelier's studies of New Mexico pueblos by instigating his own as director of the new western branch of the American School of Archaeology, headquartered in the Palace of the Governors. Hewett, Prince, and a young archaeologist named Jesse

Nusbaum restored the Palace of the Governors to its original Spanish-Pueblo architecture in 1909. They then collaborated with Colorado architect Isaac Rapp to invent Santa Fe–style architecture, which drew on Santa Fe's Pueblo and Spanish heritage.

New Mexico became a state in 1912, and began attracting artists, many of whom came to the desert to recuperate from tuberculosis contracted in industrial cities back east. Society maven Mabel Dodge Luhan in Taos and poet Witter Bynner in Santa Fe helped develop arts colonies. Each town competed to host international celebrities, such as writer D. H. Lawrence and thinker Carl Jung. Among those who returned for good was artist Georgia O'Keeffe, whose paintings have become synonymous with New Mexico for thousands of people.

During World War II, the government requisitioned the Pajarito Plateau to develop the first nuclear bomb at Los Alamos National Laboratory. Its detonation in the desert at Trinity Site and subsequent use against Japan to end World War II put lightly populated New Mexico on the map as one of the top places in the world for technological research. After the war many scientists stayed and, with a growing number of writers and artists, played an active role in New Mexico life, working for civil rights, helping to preserve Santa Fe through tough new architectural laws, and developing the arts and sciences in the southern New Mexico towns of Alamogordo and Roswell.

Visitation increased in the decades following World War II, as Route 66 gave way to fast, new interstates linking the country through Albuquerque, which became an important modern crossroads. Counter-culturalists moved to Santa Fe and Taos in the 1960s and 1970s, attracted by the same things that had brought earlier Bohemians and still attract people today: a beautiful landscape, interesting cultures, tolerance of differences, friendly small-town life, and affordable property. After magazine writers popularized Santa Fe Style in the 1980s, many of the people moving to Santa Fe were wealthy second-homers who began pricing out native-born residents. Today, however, the real challenges remain age-old: drought, scarce resources, and shifting relations among cultures.

THE PUEBLO WORLD

Navajo rugs for sale in Albuquerque. PHOTO ©CHUCK PLACE/Place Stock Photo

On May 27, 2006, the latest in New Mexico's growing roster of world-class Indian cultural centers opened at Acoma Pueblo in northwestern New Mexico. A collaboration between Indian tribal leaders and Anglo architects based in Santa Fe, Sky City Cultural Center and Haak'u Museum simultaneously manages to be both a quiet reflection of its ancient Pueblo roots and an astonishingly sophisticated, sustainable, modern building. It tells the story of the Acoma people through exhibits, films, live demonstrations and dances, workshops, regular bus tours to Sky City, and even a restaurant serving dishes inspired by traditional Pueblo foods such as corn, beans, and squash, and accompanied by modern conveniences such as Starbucks coffee.

Most important, it is one of many new Indian-owned museums in New Mexico and elsewhere whose most important role is to interpret each tribe's unique culture for its own people in its own words. Cultural centers like these, and a growing array of diverse tribal businesses, from casino-resorts, hotels, golf courses, to fishing, horseback riding, hiking, and cultural tourism, not only consolidate Indian identity and financially support Indian people but also help establish tribes as important political players in the state and beyond. Call it the Post-Modern Chaco Phenomenon.

New Mexico has 19 pueblos: Acoma, Zuni, Laguna, Sandia, Santa Ana, Jemez, Santo Domingo, Isleta, Tesuque, Pojoaque, San Ildefonso, Ohkay Owingeh (San Juan), Zia, Santa Clara, Taos, San Felipe, Nambe, Cochiti, and Picuris. The Pueblos are classified into three language groups: Zuni, Keres, and Tanoan. Zuni speaks Zuni, while the pueblos of Acoma, Cochiti, Laguna, San Felipe, Santa Ana, Santo Domingo, and Zia speak Keres. Tanoan is divided into three subcategories—Tewa, Towa, and Tiwa. Tewa-speaking pueblos include Nambe, Pojoaque, San Ildefonso, Santa Clara, Ohkay Owingeh (San Juan), and Tesuque. Tiwa-speaking pueblos include Isleta, Picuris, Sandia, and Taos. The only Towa-speaking pueblo is Jemez. The languages reflect the long migrations taken by different clans from Mesa Verde, Chaco, and elsewhere to the Rio Grande pueblos and kinship relationships established over centuries.

Acoma, Zuni, Laguna, Zia, and Santa Ana make beautiful black-on-white and polychrome pottery. San Ildefonso and Santa Clara specialize in polished red and black pots. Picuris and Taos make glittering micaceous pottery. Tesuque and Cochiti potters are known for unusual ceramic figurines such as Storyteller figures. Santo Domingo is known for its worked turquoise *heishi* (beaded disks) necklaces and other jewelry. Taos and Picuris, heavily influenced by their proximity to the Plains, make drums and leather goods like moccasins. Arts and crafts can be purchased from the Pueblos themselves or at Santa Fe's famous Indian Market in early August, the largest juried Indian art show in the world. Quality is also assured if you buy from Museum of New Mexico gift shops, under the portal at the Palace of the Governors in Santa Fe, at Eight Northern Pueblos Arts and Crafts in Ohkay Owingeh, or Indian Market.

In addition to the Pueblos, New Mexico is home to the Jicarilla Apaches of northeastern New Mexico, the Mescalero Apaches of southeastern New Mexico, and the Navajo Nation, or *Dineh*. At nearly 30,000 square miles, the Navajo Nation is the largest reservation in the country. It is spread across northwestern New Mexico, northeastern Arizona, southern Utah, and in the Checkerboard area, between Gallup and Albuquerque, where you'll find the small, noncontiguous Ramah, Alamo, and Canoncito bands. Apaches and Navajos share common roots as Athabascan hunter-gatherers from northwest Canada. The Athabascan lifestyle is a complete contrast to that of Pueblos, who are traditionally town dwellers farming fields close to multistory pueblos.

Many of the fiercely independent Navajo live in towns and cities but most retain strong connections to their reservation, where traditional tribal members observe a semi-nomadic pastoral lifestyle. Many families farm canyon bottoms and pasture sheep and goats high in the mountains in summer. They return to the rims the rest of the year, so that children can attend school, and usually live in extended family compounds consisting of a frame house, 6- to 8-sided traditional hogan, corrals, and shade ramada.

The Big Rez, as the main reservation is known, is split into 110 chapters, or local councils, represented by 88 delegates at Window Rock, the tribal capital just west of the New Mexico–Arizona border in Arizona. Outsiders are allowed to watch tribal council sessions in the historic tribal council building. You can also visit a wonderful little tribal zoo that houses animals native to the reservation, including reintroduced Mexican wolves, and learn more about Dineh history in the adjoining Navajo

Southwest pottery sampler. PHOTO ©BRUCE HUCKO

Dancers at the Taos Pueblo Powwow. PHOTO ©KERRICK JAMES

Nation Museum, a beautiful, modern, hogan-shaped building. Navajo guides offer tours here and at parks on tribal land, such as Canyon de Chelly, Navajo National Monument, Hubbell Trading Post, and Monument Valley. You can buy attractive silver jewelry, belts, handwoven wool rugs, pinyon-pitched pottery, and Navajo folk art direct from the artisans, from trading posts or from one of the seven Navajo Arts and Crafts Enterprise cooperative outlets across the Navajo Nation.

The Jicarilla Apache, clustered around the town of Dulce just south of the Colorado border, and the Mescalero Apache, headquartered near Ruidoso in southern New Mexico, were also once nomadic and today remain avid outdoorsmen. Jicarilla lands are wild and beautiful high-desert sagebrush steppe dotted with lakes at the foot of the Southern Rockies. They are mainly used for residences, grazing, hunting, fishing, camping, boating, and hiking. The tribe specializes in beadwork, baskets, paintings, and ribbon shirts, which can be purchased at the tribal arts and crafts shop in Dulce. The Mescalero Apache are renowned for their stunning reservation in the Sacramento Mountains, where they run the high-end casino-resort The Inn of the Mountain Gods, Ski Apache, Mescalero Forest Products, and the Cattle Growers Association. Navajos and Apaches are skilled horsemen. Rodeos held on the reservations are a high point of the year for native cowboys.

Cultural sensitivity is vital in New Mexico, where, if you're Anglo, you'll often be in the minority. Here are some things to bear in mind. Native American is a recent, politically correct Anglo term. It's fine to use the term "Indian" or better yet a person's tribal affiliation, e.g.

Laguna, Taos, Jemez, or Picuris Pueblo, Jicarilla Apache, or Navajo. When visiting Indian pueblos and reservations, which are sovereign nations within the United States, behave respectfully. Don't use racist terms.

Abide by all rules and regulations, including prohibitions on photography, sketching, taking notes, video, and audio recording. If photography is permitted, a fee may be required. If you wish to take an individual's picture, you must ask permission first (a gratuity may be requested). Respect all restricted areas; these are usually posted. You'll usually need a permit to hike, hunt, fish, or drive around on back roads on Indian land.

Never enter a home unless invited. Remember you are a guest on Indian land. Be polite and accommodating. Don't ask intrusive questions or interrupt during ceremonies or dances. Even if an Indian event is not explicitly religious (such as a pow-wow), it may have a spiritual component. Show the same respect at Indian ceremonies that you would at any other religious service. At all events, try to maintain a low profile, both in manner, conversation, and in dress (cover up and avoid shorts, bare arms, and flipflops). Keep in mind that ceremonies and Pueblo dances aren't performances scheduled for public viewing, and you may attend only at the discretion of the tribe. Applause and talking are not appropriate.

Call ahead to make sure ceremonies, powwows, and other events are taking place and prepare for long delays once there: Indians usually work by consensus and things tend to happen only when elders consider the time is right or preparations are complete.

Finally, it is polite to accept if you are invited to eat in an Indian home. Extending hospitality to visitors and feeding them well is a long Indian tradition. Never offend your hosts by offering to pay for the food, and once you are finished eating, be sure to leave the table promptly. Many others will be fed that day.

For more information, contact Albuquerque's excellent Indian Pueblo Cultural Center (2401 12th St. SW, Albuquerque; 505-843-7270), which has exhibits on New Mexico's 19 pueblos, scheduled dance and craft demonstrations, and a restaurant serving Pueblo foods.

Santa Fe, Taos, and Albuquerque

Church of St. Francis of Assisi, Rancho de Taos. PHOTO ©KERRICK JAMES

SANTA FE was founded sometime between 1603 and 1610 and is the oldest capital in the country. Four flags have flown over the Palace of the Governors, the 400-year-old adobe administrative building on the north side of the Plaza: Spanish, Mexican, American, and (briefly during the Civil War) Confederate. The Palace has housed 60 Spanish, Mexican, and American governors; occupying Pueblo Indians between 1680 and 1692; soldiers from nearby Fort Marcy; a jail; a post office; the School of American Archaeology (now the School for Advanced Research); and the New Mexico Historical Society. Today, the Palace of the Governors is home to the Museum of New Mexico history museum.

Santa Fe has four historic districts and 3,500 listed buildings protected by one of the most powerful historical review boards in the country. A $15, four-day pass to the Museum of New Mexico allows entry to five museums (two downtown and three on Museum Hill, off Old Santa Fe Trail) and is the city's best bargain. For information on individual MNM units, see the Beyond the Parks section in the back of the book. They are free Fridays from 5–8 p.m. and to New Mexico residents on Sundays.

If you're new to Santa Fe, it's well worth the extra cost to stay downtown. Nowhere else will you enter the spirit of Santa Fe so completely and be able to see as much in as short a time without driving. Begin a walking tour of historic downtown Santa Fe at the Plaza, after picking up information from the main Santa Fe Visitor Center on the corner of Old Santa Fe Trail and Paseo de Peralta, across from the State Capitol. The visitor center is next door to the photogenic San Miguel Mission. Santa Fe's oldest church, this chapel is known for its old bell and early paintings on bison hide.

Although it is less of the daily community meeting place it once was, the Plaza remains a popular place for socializing, free music and dancing in the Gazebo in summer, Indian and Spanish Markets in July and August, and holiday events such as a traditional reenactment of Mary and Joseph's search for lodging (Las Posadas) at Christmas. Narrow, winding streets radiating from the Plaza lead to many important downtown attractions.

On San Francisco Street, you'll find La Posada, the famous historic "inn at the end of the Santa Fe Trail"; the 1931 Lensic Center for Performing Arts, on the site of a popular gaming house and brothel run by Doña Tules, one of Santa Fe's infamous 19th-century "liberated women"; Gothic-style St. Francis Cathedral Basilica; and the nearby Loretto Chapel, which has a circular staircase that seems to rise without any support. The Loretto Chapel was built in the late 1800s by infamous French-born Archbishop Lamy, the controversial subject of Willa Cather's novel *Death Comes for the Archbishop*.

Santa Fe is no longer caught in the timewarp it once was. The iconoclastic Institute of Indian Arts (IAIA) Museum, opposite St. Francis Cathedral, at the end of East San Francisco Street, is affiliated with the IAIA, also in Santa Fe, which has trained emerging Indian artists since the 1930s. Housed in the old adobe post office, it contains one of the world's largest collections of cutting-edge American Indian art.

An emerging new community center can be found in the Historic Railyards off Guadalupe Street, a few blocks northwest of the Plaza. Historic Southern Railway offers daily train rides to Lamy, location of the main Amtrak link. SITE Santa Fe, housed in a former warehouse, specializes in avant-garde art, while El Museo Cultural, a grassroots museum, interprets Hispanic history in the Americas.

Santa Fe Farmers Market, a popular local institution for 40 years and one of the top 10 farmers markets in the nation, will be open year round by early 2008 in its own building in the vibrant new multi-use 13-acre Railyard Park and Plaza just off Guadalupe Street. Support means that new generations of family farmers can continue farming in northern New Mexico and keep alive the state's ancient *acequia* (irrigation ditch) system, which dates back centuries.

The Acequia Madre (the Mother Ditch) is located off East Alameda, a pleasant cottonwood-shaded walk along the intermittent Santa Fe River. Tiny galleries throng nearby Canyon Road, the traditional road from Sante Fe through the mountains to Pecos Pueblo, 25 miles away. This is Santa Fe's loveliest historic neighborhood. Upper Canyon Road continues to trails at the Audubon Center and Santa Fe Preserve, next to the reservoirs that provide drinking water for Santa Fe. If you really want a walk, head south on Camino del Monte Sol, filled with historic artist homes, to reach museums on Museum Hill.

TAOS

Funky Taos, adjoining Taos Pueblo on a plateau between the Rio Grande Gorge and Wheeler Peak, the state's highest mountain, has a long history of attracting creative, idiosyncratic people like mountain man Kit Carson, socialites Mabel Dodge Luhan and Millicent Rogers, writer D. H. Lawrence, and artists who founded the state's first art colony in 1898. In the Sixties, it attracted hippies like actor Dennis Hopper who wanted to get back to the land. Many are still there, and have placed their own unique stamp on the town that many say is "what Santa Fe used to be like."

Begin on Kit Carson Road, where you'll find Kit Carson Home and Museum, used by the famed scout and Indian fighter and his family from 1843 to 1868. Fellow mountain man Charles Bent, the first US Territorial governor in 1848 lived on nearby Bent Street. He was murdered in an uprising in 1849. Heading through the quiet plaza, with its shops selling traditional arts and crafts, continue to several interesting art museums located on Ledoux Street, off Camino de la Placita. The first, R. C. Gorman Gallery, showcases the work of the late Navajo artist. A few doors down is the E. L. Blumenschein Home and Museum, the modest adobe home of artist Ernest Blumenschein who, along with artist Bert Phillips, arrived here in 1898 and organized the Taos Society of Artists.

Taos Society artists Blumenstein, Phillips, Victor Higgins, John Marin, Marsden Hartley, and Dorothy Brett are displayed at the nearby Harwood Museum of Art, the second-oldest museum in the state. Another good collection can be found in the Taos Art Museum, which is on display in the former home of Russian-born artist Nicholai Fechin, who carved the wood inside this lovely building.

A few miles northwest of downtown is the Millicent Rogers Museum, which contains extraordinary Indian jewelry, textiles, and art, including an important collection by famed San Ildefonso potter Maria Martinez and her family. Continue on US 64 to visit the dramatic Rio Grande Gorge Bridge, the second highest suspension bridge in the nation; Taos Ski Valley is east of US 64, on NM 150. Continue on US 64 to drive the Enchanted Circle scenic drive, which circles the mountains, coming out south of Taos. The scenic drive includes a visit to the D. H. Lawrence Ranch, where the famous writer, his wife Frieda, and several friends lived a back-to-the-land existence. Taos Pueblo, the town's biggest attraction, is worth a special trip. Occupied since A.D. 1000, the main pueblo is stunning against its mountain backdrop. In the Old Pueblo, you can buy moccasins, micaceous pottery, beadwork, and Taos's famous drums, which can be heard all over town.

ALBUQUERQUE

In 2006, Albuquerque celebrated the 300th anniversary of its founding by Spanish colonists on the site of an old *estancia*, or ranch. The lively historic Plaza in Old Town is similar to Santa Fe's Plaza but more Mexican in feel. Christmas is the time to visit 1793 San Felipe de Negri Church, which is bathed in candlelight from thousands of brown bag *farolito* lanterns lighting the way for the Christ Child.

Albuquerque's "museum row" is just around the corner on Mountain Road. The Albuquerque Museum of Art and History chronicles Albuquerque history, including exhibits on *vaqueros*, or Spanish cowboys, and art by Taos Society artists, Georgia O'Keeffe, and Mexican-born fiberglass sculptor Luis Jimenez, who died in 2006. Explora Science Center and the New Mexico Museum of Natural History and Science are geared

Palace Avenue and Palace of the Governors. PHOTO ©KERRICK JAMES

San Miguel Mission, late afternoon. PHOTO ©CHUCK PLACE/Place Stock Photo

Colorful mail boxes along Canyon Road. PHOTO ©CHUCK PLACE/Place Stock Photo

Church of San Geronimo, Taos Pueblo. PHOTO ©CHUCK PLACE/Place Stock Photo

Taos Pueblo. PHOTO ©KERRICK JAMES

Albuquerque Balloon Festival. PHOTO ©CHUCK PLACE/Place Stock Photo

Route 66 Diner, Central Avenue, Albuquerque. PHOTO ©KERRICK JAMES

toward kids. The latter, with its dinosaur skeletons, dynamic geology exhibit, Dynomax Theater, and Lodestar Planetarium, is THE best place to learn about New Mexico's volcanoes, dinosaurs, and astronomy. The Rio Grande Zoo, Aquarium, and Botanical Garden—together called the BioPark—are also kid friendly.

The Indian Pueblo Cultural Center, off Rio Grande Boulevard at 12th and Menaul, is a great place to learn more about the state's 19 Indian pueblos and watch dancing. Fabulous pottery by the Mimbres branch of the Mogollon culture is exhibited at the superb Maxwell Anthropology Museum on the UNM campus off Central Avenue, a major segment of Route 66. Route 66 heads west through the recently renovated downtown, where nostalgia buffs will enjoy the many neon-lit establishments.

There are many recreational opportunities in the Sandia Mountains and along the Rio Grande, which bisects the city. Albuquerque's most important event, Balloon Fiesta, takes place in the north Rio Grande Valley at Balloon Fiesta Park. Hotels in Albuquerque and Santa Fe usually sell out for the Balloon Fiesta in October. The same is true for the New Mexico State Fair in September, which features nightly rodeos with concerts by nationally famous music groups. Book early.

Red Mesa and colorful badlands near Abiquiu.

GEORGIA O'KEEFFE

The painter whose bold, sensuous depictions of bones, flowers, hills, and adobe buildings are synonymous with New Mexico for many moved here permanently in 1948, late in a very successful art career in New York City. She first visited in 1929, as a guest of Taos socialite Mabel Dodge Luhan. She was drawn immediately to the Chama River valley. It was, she wrote her husband Alfred Stieglitz, an influential photographer and gallery owner in New York City, "perfectly mad-looking country—hills and cliffs and washes too crazy to imagine all thrown up into the air by God and let tumble where they would."

O'Keeffe was born in Wisconsin in 1888. A beautiful and striking woman, she trained at the Art Institute of Chicago, then moved to New York, where she was "discovered" in 1916 by Stieglitz, who became her mentor, lover, and finally her husband. O'Keeffe lived in Texas for several years, where she taught school in a rural farming community not unlike the one she had grown up in in the Midwest.

Her 1929 trip to New Mexico began nearly three decades of summer painting trips to the state. She quickly tired of the meddling intensity of Mabel Dodge, a frustrated artist and writer, and the art colonies in Santa Fe and Taos. She based herself, instead, in the colorful eroded Colorado Plateau country around Abiquiu, at a dude ranch called Ghost Ranch, owned by publisher Arthur Pack, who loaned her an adobe home for her use and sold it to her in 1940.

After Pack donated the dude ranch to the Presbyterian Church as a conference and retreat center, O'Keeffe continued to summer at Ghost Ranch and talked the Catholic Church into selling her a ruined 18th-century *hacienda* in Abiquiu, which, with the help of friend Marie Cabot, she renovated and moved to in 1949. From then on, she summered at Ghost Ranch and wintered in Abiquiu, until ill health forced her to move to Santa Fe in 1984. She died there in 1986 at the age of 98.

The wildly popular Georgia O'Keeffe Museum in downtown Santa Fe opened in 1997. Ten minimalist, white-walled galleries feature a video about O'Keeffe, revolving exhibits of O'Keeffe's work between 1916 and 1980, and special shows. One-hour tours of the O'Keeffe Home in Abiquiu are available by reservation only (505-685-4539) Tuesday, Thursday, and Friday, April to November. Tours begin at the offices of the Georgia O'Keeffe Foundation, across the street in the Abiquiu Inn; group limit is 12 people.

OPPOSITE: The Rio Chama as it flows between Abiquiu and Ghost Ranch. PHOTO ©TIM FITZHARRIS

AZTEC
NATIONAL MONUMENT

The reconstructed Great Kiva. PHOTO ©GEORGE H.H. HUEY

It's late afternoon on a winter's day on the banks of the Animas River in northeastern New Mexico. The sandstone walls of the sprawling 12th-century multistory pueblo complex of Aztec Ruins glow red-gold as the sun sets. A few remaining visitors pause to take photos on the 800-yard trail through the stabilized West Ruin, the largest of three Chacoan great house pueblos at the monument. It was built between A.D. 1109 and the early 1120s, as impressive as any similar public structure in Chaco Canyon, the cultural center to the southwest from which it sprang.

Camera lenses pick out elements in the walls highlighted by the lengthening shadows. T-shaped doorways lead into room suites in the protected interior of the 400-room, three-story structure. An unusual 13th-century triwalled kiva, one of three on the 27-acre monument, sits north of West Ruin. Triwalled kivas—a northern San Juan phenomenon—are still an enigmatic presence in former Chaco sites reoccupied by later Mesas Verdeans. This one was excavated by archaeologist Gordon Vivian, but its use is still unclear.

Rare for a different reason is the 41-foot reconstructed great kiva, or community ceremonial structure, in the central plaza of West Ruin. It's the only such structure in the National Park System, a hushed, cathedral-like space with massive supports holding up the roof, where the original ladder entryway allows in a shaft of light that pools on the packed dirt floor. It offers a unique opportunity to enter the type of ceremonial room still used by the modern Pueblo descendants of the Chaco and later Mesa Verde people. Ancestral Puebloans had left the Four Corners region and moved to the Rio Grande and Little Colorado river drainages by A.D. 1300, most likely due to a long-running drought, colder and shorter growing seasons, and environmental overuse.

Workmanlike, Mesa Verde-style walls of even, bricklike slabs of sandstone secured with large quantities of mud mortar sit cheek-by-jowl with elegant Chacoan walls laid out like a mosaic, their tightly packed stones chinked with smaller pebbles. One Chaco mason even included a decorative band of greenish stones around a *viga* roof beam. The smooth plaster that once concealed this artistry is long gone, but what lies hidden, the Chacoan builders seem to say, is as important as what you see on the surface. "God," as one architect once said, "is in the details."

Aztec appeared on this tributary of the San Juan River just as the phenomenonally successful Chaco civilization began its slide toward the diaspora that would force whole villages of starving people to scatter all over the Four Corners. One of the largest of a number of preplanned great house complexes in the 25,000-square-mile San Juan Basin, Aztec was ordered built by leaders who were attracted by the ready source of irrigation and fertile soils. The three great houses probably served as redistribution, trade, and ceremonial centers for a large, expanded population of 100 smaller pueblos in the valley and on the river terraces whose residents had built and maintained them.

Today, only West Ruin, excavated by archaeologist Earl Morris between 1916 and 1923, is open to the public. Morris concluded that Aztec was only used by Chacoans for a few decades, then stood empty for about 25 years until reoccupied by people from Mesa Verde. Modern archaeologists, using more sophisticated dating methods, believe the Aztec region was never completely abandoned. Instead, a transitional culture existed here that eventually exhibited Mesa Verde cultural traits.

Aztec Ruins National Monument adjoins the modern town of Aztec, off US 550. It is open daily and has a small museum displaying pottery, yucca sandals, and other artifacts, as well as a gift shop. A film on the Ancestral Pueblo people is shown throughout the day, and a self-guided tour booklet explains features in West Ruin. In addition, there are occasional cultural demonstrations and scholarly lectures in summer, daily ranger talks, and occasional weekend tours of unexcavated East Ruin.

BANDELIER
NATIONAL MONUMENT

Overview of Tyuonyi Pueblo, Frijoles Canyon. PHOTO ©TOM DANIELSEN

They came to Bandelier from the Four Corners—refugees from the Chaco and Mesa Verde cultures, two successful Ancestral Pueblo civilizations that had, by turns, dominated the Southwest between A.D. 900 and 1300. They brought with them many technologies: masonry architecture villages, decorated ceramics, irrigated farming, woven cotton, and a ceremonial tradition that included seasonal astronomical observations of the heavens. Chaco leaders had lived in great houses in the San Juan Basin, eaten the best food, and orchestrated a thriving economy based on trade. Mesa Verde people, also traders, had built protected villages in the cliffs and atop the well-watered headlands of southwestern Colorado. Yet none of their ingenuity could prevent these cultures from having to move on when a series of long-lasting droughts hit. Nature, after all, still had the upper hand.

Clansfolk headed southeast to the Pajarito Plateau, the east-facing slopes of the 10,000-foot Jemez Mountains above the Rio Grande. As long ago as 11,000 B.C., these cool uplands had been used by transient Clovis and Folsom people. They hunted bison and mammoth until a warming trend (and perhaps their hunting efficiency) doomed the big game. Their successors, the Archaic, were more sedentary, hunting and gathering seasonally for edible plant species such as piñon nuts and wild grasses and game such as deer and elk. They lived in semi-subterranean pithouses that were cool in summer and warm in winter. Their descendants, the Ancestral Pueblo people, would later modify snug pithouses into communal ceremonial rooms, or kivas, beneath above ground room blocks, a living link between past and present.

For millennia, people had been attracted to the Jemez Mountains by the hard, sharp-edged obsidian produced by the volcanic eruption that had formed the mountains just over a million years earlier. Prehistoric people treasured obsidian for flaked spear points, arrowheads, and tools, and Chaco and Mesa Verde people had long traveled to the region to trade for it. Now successive generations left their used-up villages in the Four Corners and migrated along the trade route to the Rio Grande—this time to start over.

The first Chacoan immigrants arrived in Frijoles Canyon around A.D. 1150. In the bottom of Frijoles Canyon, the year-round Frijoles Creek provided water for farming and drinking. Homes were a creative mixture of the old and the new: small masonry pueblos built directly against south-facing cliffs of volcanic tuff, a soft material that could be carved with simple basaltic tools into hundreds of cave rooms (cavates). Men wove cotton on looms hung from the ceiling, and women began making distinctive black-on-gray pottery, creating finely crafted jars and bowls inspired by their new homeland.

In the late 1200s, a new wave of Four Corners refugees built Tyuonyi, a large pueblo on the canyon floor housing 100 people. As available living space on the plateau diminished, residents moved from small hamlets occupied by families for a generation into larger, longer-lived villages of room blocks built around a central plaza. These larger, multistory pueblos were economically sustainable, occupying a small footprint and opening up surrounding lands for farming.

Ancestral Pueblo people once again pooled their resources, improving architecture and agricultural practices. But the old political hierarchy that had doomed Chaco and Mesa Verde never again took root. Pueblos were now split either into clans or moieties (tribal subdivisions), which took charge of winter and summer ceremonials. Each pueblo developed specialized crafts that it traded with neighboring pueblos in the region.

By the 1500s, a cooling trend, growing populations, and scarce resources triggered another migration—this time closer to home. Groups linked by their shared Keres or Tewa languages and traditions moved to warmer lowlands and began building autonomous pueblos along the Rio Grande, using lands from the river to the mountains. This is where Pajarito Plateau descendants—the Cochiti, Santa Clara, San Ildefonso, San Felipe, and Santo Domingo people—still live today, with Zuñi Pueblo also maintaining a strong link to the area. The almost 3,000 archaeological sites in Bandelier National Monument are their ancestral homelands, providing an unbroken link to the past.

It was a Cochiti Pueblo man, Juan Jose Montoya, who in 1880 first showed the cliff dwellings in Frijoles Canyon to Adolph Bandelier, the self-taught Swiss ethnographer and archaeologist for whom the national monument was named in 1916. "It was the grandest thing I ever saw," said Bandelier. In the early 1900s, another self-taught archaeologist, Dr. Edgar Lee Hewett, director of the Las Vegas Normal School, spent

Ladder and kiva at Alcove House. PHOTO ©GEORGE H.H. HUEY

Ladder and cave entries above Long House. PHOTO ©TOM TILL

Upper Falls on Frijole Creek. PHOTO ©LAURENCE PARENT

Detail view of Long House and volcanic cliff with caves. PHOTO ©BRUCE HUCKO

several summers excavating on the Pajarito Plateau with his students. The well-connected Hewett was instrumental in establishing Bandelier National Monument, using the 1906 Antiquities Act, which he had written and helped get signed into law.

In 1925, Evelyn and George Frey and their son Richard came to Frijoles Canyon to manage a guest ranch. Then, in 1933, the Civilian Conservation Corps (CCC) arrived to build an entrance road and new stone park buildings. Frijoles Canyon Lodge (now the park gift shop, snack bar, and administrative buildings) was built in 1939-40, and Evelyn stayed on to run it until her retirement in 1978. The old ranch buildings were pulled down around 1940. Bandelier has the largest concentration of CCC structures, furnishings, and tinwork and some of the best WPA art in the National Park System.

The easy 1.2-mile Main Loop Trail along the bottom of Frijoles Canyon begins behind the visitor center, visiting Tyuonyi Pueblo and cliff dwellings, continuing an additional mile round trip to Alcove House, a cliff dwelling reached by climbing three long ladders. The moderate Falls Trail leads to two waterfalls above the Rio Grande and offers a look into the volcanic history of the monument, while the Frey Trail links the canyon with the pleasant Juniper Campground on the mesa top. Seventy percent of Bandelier is designated wilderness, with many opportunities for solitude on backcountry trails that are home to endangered species such as the Jemez Mountain salamander.

Cave dwellings and ladder above Long House, Bandelier National Monument.

ADOLPH BANDELIER

Famed 19th-century New Mexico archaeologist Adolph Bandelier was born in Berne, Switzerland, in 1840 and moved to Illinois with his family in 1848. While growing up, he was a keen naturalist and returned to Berne in 1855 to study geology. He developed a passion for anthropology during the Civil War while working in an office. After reading extensively about North American history and ethnology in his spare time, he studied several languages, including the old form of Spanish, in order to be able to read historic documents in their original language.

He maintained an ongoing correspondence with anthropologist Lewis Henry Morgan, whose theories on social evolution later influenced Friedrich Engles and Karl Marx. Under Morgan's tutelage, beginning in 1877, Bandelier wrote an important series of monographs on the political organization of the Aztec culture through the Peabody Museum of Harvard. He had never even been to Mexico.

Wanderlust caught up with Bandelier in 1880, when, with the help of Morgan, Frederic W. Putnam, Charles Eliot Norton, and the newly formed Archaeological Institute of America, he received funding for the AIA's first project in American archaeology: the social organization, usages, and customs of the Pueblo tribes of the Southwest and the architecture of the structures they occupied. The project was suggested by Lewis Henry Morgan, who felt that the most important Pueblo sites to be studied lay in the Four Corners, where Colorado, Utah, Arizona, and New Mexico join.

For the next five years, Bandelier devoted himself to his subject, traveling constantly throughout New Mexico, mostly on foot. "I have known many scholars and some heroes," declared journalist and fellow Southwest adventurer Charles Lummis. "But they seldom come in the same package." Bandelier's 1890 report was widely read. In it, he called attention to the escalating loss of antiquities at pueblo sites such as Pecos, of which he wrote, "the vandalism committed to this venerable relic of antiquity defies all description."

The report led directly to the founding of the School of American Archaeology, the western branch of the AIA in Santa Fe. Its director, archaeologist Edgar Lee Hewett, admired Bandelier's earlier work. He undertook a survey of archaeological sites on the Pajarito Plateau at the turn of the century, excavated Frijoles Canyon between 1907 and 1914, and, based on the sheer quantity of archaeological sites recorded, recommended the entire Pajarito Plateau be set aside as a national park. In 1916, a decade after the Antiquities Act had been enacted allowing presidential proclamation of national monuments with congressional approval, a much smaller national monument, centered on Frijoles Canyon, was set aside as Bandelier National Monument by President Wilson, honoring Bandelier's early contribution to archaeology in New Mexico.

OPPOSITE: Trail worn into volcanic tuff at Tsankawi Unit of Bandelier National Monument. PHOTO ©BRUCE HUCKO

CAPULIN
VOLCANIC NATIONAL MONUMENT

Capulin Volcano, summer storm at sunset. PHOTO ©WILLIAM STONE

The 8,000-square-mile Raton-Clayton Volcanic Field in northeastern New Mexico, where the Rocky Mountains meet the High Plains, is the easternmost Cenozoic-Era volcanic field in the nation. Its star attraction is Capulin Volcano, a splendid cinder cone set aside as a national monument in 1916. Capulin stands about 1,000 feet above the surrounding prairie grassland and is flanked by a series of four lava flows covering 15.7 miles around the base of the cone.

Capulin is an archetypal cinder cone and is also one of America's most accessible volcanoes. A winding, two-mile, paved historic road is open year round and leads to two paved walking trails. The 0.2-mile-long Crater Vent Trail provides a rare opportunity to descend into the crater. The mile-long Crater Rim Trail rises slowly in elevation to the 8,182-foot summit (about 400 feet elevation gain) as it circles the rim. It offers amazing 360-degree views of surrounding volcanoes and four states: New Mexico, Texas, Colorado, and Oklahoma.

Capulin was built by a series of eruptions that spewed lava and fiery cinders from a volcanic vent. After the first major eruption, four separate lava flows oozed from vents in the volcano's *boca,* or mouth, at the base of the crater, protecting the symmetry of the cone. Initial comparison dating with alluvium sites indicated that Capulin erupted contemporaneously with local inhabitation by Folsom Man (10,000 years before present). This error was exposed in 1996, when argon-argon dating of Capulin's rocks pushed back the eruption date to 56,000–62,000 years ago.

Capulin's eruption marked the final phase (between 1.7 million and 30,000 years ago) of about nine million years of activity in the Raton-Clayton Volcanic Field. In the western portion of the field, 8,422-foot Red Mountain and 8,818-foot Laughlin Peak are lava domes pushed up by extrusion of highly viscous magma during the Raton Phase (9.0 to 3.5 million years ago). This type of magma is too thick to form a lava flow. Dominating the southeast is 8,720-foot Sierra Grande, an andesitic shield volcano that began building during the Clayton Phase (2.25 to 3.0 million years ago). Most andesitic volcanoes are composite volcanoes, like Mount St. Helens, while shield volcanoes are basaltic, like those in Hawaii. Sierra Grande is neither a true shield volcano nor a true composite volcano. To the north, 7,190-foot Mud Hill is a *maar,* where lava hit groundwater while erupting, causing a highly explosive steam-driven eruption during the Capulin Phase.

Colorful lichens soften the appearance of the volcanic rocks on Capulin, and secrete acid that helps break them up into rich soil, allowing dense piñon pine, juniper, and ponderosa pine to root in the volcano's steep sides. Woody shrubs, grasses, and wildflowers form the understory here. Shrubs include mountain mahogany, Gambel oak, and the abundant chokecherry, whose Spanish name, *capulin,* gave the volcano its name. Capulin's red-and-black slopes and base are transformed in the spring and summer months by spectacular wildflowers. Prickly poppy, primrose, goldenrod, sunflowers, and Indian paintbrush nestle among native shortgrass prairie grasses such as bluestem, threeawn, grama, and squirreltail. Fall's cooler temperatures alter the show, allowing the red-and-orange blocks of Gambel oak to take their turn onstage for a final showstopping flameout before winter sets in.

The volcanoes are only a small part of the whole field. Mesa tops capped by Raton Phase columnar lava flows date from 7.7 to 5 million years old. Normal geological pattern would put these flows below other layers, but reverse topography occurred when lava flowed into river valleys carved from sedimentary rock, filling them. The uncapped sedimentary rock eroded faster than the lava flow and created mesas. The process was repeated as younger volcanoes erupted and new flows again filled low-lying areas. One of these mesas—45-mile-long Black Mesa in Oklahoma—is the northeasternmost feature in the Raton-Clayton Volcanic Field. Black Mesa Nature Preserve, at the top of 4,973-foot Black Mesa, is the highest point in Oklahoma. Sugarite Canyon State Park, near Raton, preserves a portion of the columnar-jointed, Pliocene-Age basalt flows that cap the high mesas in the park area. Good camping can be found in the state park. Gas, food, and lodging are available in Raton.

OPPOSITE: Capulin Volcano and volcanic debris seen from the North. PHOTO ©GEORGE H.H. HUEY

CARLSBAD
CAVERNS NATIONAL PARK

Spelunker in Ogle Cave, Carlsbad Caverns National Park. PHOTO ©LAURENCE PARENT

When the thermometer hits 100 degrees in the Chihuahuan Desert of southeastern New Mexico in summer, many desert creatures stay cool underground until nightfall. The closest thing for humans is Carlsbad Cavern, which acts like a cold trap where the temperature falls to an unusually low 56 degrees Fahrenheit all year. The temperature within the more than 100 other known caves remains around 68 degrees.

Thirty miles of cave passages have been explored within Carlsbad Cavern, including the Big Room, one of the largest cave rooms in the United States, occupying an area equal in size to 6.2 football fields and as much as 24 stories high. Spectacular limestone decorations, or speleothems, line every surface. Soda straws, daggerlike stalactites, wavy helictites, fragile aragonite, and draperies form eerily translucent decorations on dripping walls and ceilings. Stalagmites rear up from the floor like great melting candles. Conjoined stalactites and stalagmites soar into mighty columns that look like they're holding up the roof of the room. Calcite "lily pads" formed on now-dry crystalline lakes dammed by flowstone. Pools hold nests of "cave pearls." And due to a very complex system of convection currents you'll find more "popcorn" than in any movie theater.

Painted designs (pictographs) on the walls at the cave entrance may indicate use by early Mescalero Apache, who roasted agave hearts in pits. Spanish colonists of the 16th century who followed a Pecos River route some distance from these mountains probably missed these formations. In the darkness blind centipedes evolved. Most visible, though, is the large colony of migratory Brazilian free-tailed bats that roost in the summer in the Bat Cave, near the Natural Entrance, 200 feet below the earth's surface. An unforgettable sight, they whir out of the cave mouth to feed at dusk in huge black clouds, then return to roosts each dawn in a tremendous buzzing of folding wings, as they plummet into the depths.

Local settlers began harvesting bat guano to sell as fertilizer to California citrus groves in 1903, but cowboy Jim White was the first to discover Carlsbad's inner secrets. Legend has it that he was fixing a fenceline and thought he saw smoke in the distance. Moving closer, he realized he was watching bats flying out of a cave entrance. Curious, White returned later to explore the cave, using a lariat (a cowboy's rope) to climb down inside and a miner's lamp whose weak glow illuminated

Carlsbad's otherworldly ambiance. White was soon giving tours of the caves by letting visitors down in guano buckets. Sometime between 1915 and 1917, he led photographer Ray Davis into the caves. The ensuing photos drew great publicity. Carlsbad was set aside as a national monument in 1923, upgraded to a national park in 1930, and became a World Heritage Site in 1995.

Carlsbad's complex cave system has its origins in the 400-mile-long, horseshoe-shaped living reef that grew in an arm of a warm, tropical, inland sea in Permian times, 250 million years ago. As sponges and calcareous algae died in the shallows, lime secretions from their skeletons and seawater hardened into Capitan Reef Limestone. Later, the sea became landlocked and evaporated, leaving behind deep deposits of gypsum, salt, and potash that buried the reef. It did not reemerge until a period of intensive mountain building in the West 70 million years ago created the Guadalupe Mountains. Basin-and-range faulting tilted the mountains between 20 and 5 million years ago and accelerated the erosion that uncovered the reef.

The caves began forming between three and 11 million years ago, after the uplift of the Guadalupe Mountains began. The main sculptor was sulfuric acid, formed by the mixing of fresh water from above and deeper, hydrogen-sulfide-rich water from below. The speolothems may have begun forming while the hollowing process was still going on in lower levels. Water moving through cracks encountered drier air in the caves, dropped its carbon dioxide load and evaporated, leaving behind precipitated calcite-crystalline formations that line the main cave and the chambers leading off it. The last ice age, which ended 10,000 years ago, is believed to be the last major period of speleothem activity.

Tiny, ricelike fossils known as fusilinids are etched in bas-relief on Iceberg Rock in the Main Corridor. They are a type of foraminifera, a key feature of the Permian era. The mass extinction of the Permian era, the greatest in the fossil record, wiped out fusilinids and many trilobites, ammonites, nautiloids, and brachiopods. Carlsbad Caverns preserves one of the best exposures of Permian-era fossil reefs in the world. Lechuguilla Cave—discovered in 1986 and only open to qualified researchers and trained explorers with cave mapping skills—continues to offer scientists unique research opportunities. Its biota has been examined as a possible

Draperies on wall of The Big Room. PHOTO ©ROBERT HILDEBRAND

Huge stalagmite in The Big Room known as Giant Dome. PHOTO ©TOM TILL

Stalactites, stalagmites, and columns in The Big Room. PHOTO ©ROBERT HILDEBRAND

The "Clansman" formation in Slaughter Canyon Cave PHOTO ©LAURENCE PARENT

model of life on Mars. Even more exciting are the cancer-destroying bacteria that have been discovered, offering new possibilities for treating the disease.

Visitors walk the 1.25-mile Big Room on a self-guided tour, viewing such highlights as the Hall of Giants, the Bottomless Pit, and the Rock of Ages. Access is via a one-minute elevator ride from the visitor center or by hiking the Natural Entrance Trail, a steep, 800-foot descent. King's Palace Tour visits four highly decorated chambers not on the usual self-guided route. In summer, daily off-trail adventure tours, led by park rangers and limited in size, offer a taste of wild caving for an additional fee. Lower Cave Tour includes climbing up and down ladders, and walking and crawling through passageways. The candlelit lantern tour of Left Hand Tunnel highlights Carlsbad's colorful human history. Most popular is the 1.25-mile Slaughter Canyon Cave Tour, which requires climbing a strenuous half-mile trail to the cave entrance and visits one of the world's largest limestone columns. Reserve all guided tours in advance by calling (877) 444-6777. Rattlesnake Springs, a protected riparian area of the 73-square-mile park, has picnic tables. White's City and Carlsbad have the closest food and lodging. The nearest park service campground is Pine Springs in nearby Guadalupe Mountains National Park, a drive of about 45 miles. Arrive early in summer to get a spot.

PAGE 44/45: Totem Pole and Chandelier in The Big Room. PHOTO ©LARRY ULRICH

CHACO
CULTURE NATIONAL HISTORICAL PARK

Meticulous masonry of Pueblo Bonito. PHOTO ©EDUARDO FUSS

In 1895, when Richard Wetherill guided the Palmer family from Kansas to view the spectacular ancient stone buildings in 15-mile-long Chaco Canyon, the cowboy-archaeologist was already famous for his excavation of Mesa Verde. A year later, Wetherill, ex-Harvard student George Pepper, and their mainly Navajo crew drove a supply wagon through the high-desert sagebrush to the canyon, set up a tent camp behind the largest and most beautiful of the buildings, Pueblo Bonito, and over the next three summers, mapped, recorded, and excavated 190 rooms.

In the first season alone, they uncovered 114 unusual cylinder-shaped black-on-white pots in just one room, a quiver containing 81 arrows, more than 375 carved wooden staffs that may have been prayer sticks, a cylindrical basket encrusted with mosaic and turquoise shell, six wooden flutes, stone effigies of birds, frogs, and tadpoles, some inlaid with turquoise, and huge quantities of raw and worked turquoise. Boxcar loads of priceless artifacts were then freighted back east, where they would eventually end up in the American Museum of Natural History in New York City.

In 1900, Santa Fe's School for Advanced Research founder Edgar Lee Hewett alerted the U.S. Government to the Hyde Exploring Expedition's activities, shut the operation down, then helped draft legislation for the landmark 1906 Antiquities Act, which allows the President to protect cultural treasures by designating them national monuments. In 1907, Chaco Canyon was one of the first such sites to be set aside. In 1980, after archaeologists discovered an extensive road system leading from Chaco Canyon throughout the 25,000-square-mile San Juan Basin, it was upgraded to Chaco Culture National Historical Park. Today, it is a World Heritage Site, significant for what it tells us about the history of mankind.

A paved scenic loop leads to Chetro Ketl, Pueblo Bonito, and Pueblo Del Arroyo, the major pueblos on the north side of the canyon; two 12th-century pueblos, Casa Chiquita and Kin Kletso, lie along the old entry road into the canyon, now closed to vehicles. The loop then returns to the visitor center via the great kiva of Casa Rinconada, the largest in the canyon, and its associated small village sites across from Pueblo Bonito. Hiking trails above and below the cliffs then lead to backcountry pueblos such as Pueblo Alto, Tsin Kletzin, Wijiji, and Peñasco Blanco, which probably served as communication stations for travelers arriving at Chaco from across the San Juan Basin.

Even in ruined form, shored up on crutches like a patient on life support, Pueblo Bonito was clearly the center of the Chacoan world, the mother of all Chacoan great houses—massive, overbuilt public buildings that feature multistoried construction, distinctive masonry, large rooms built around a central plaza, and oversized subterranean ceremonial chambers, or great kivas (one of Pueblo Bonito's most memorable features is its three great kivas and 30 small kivas).

Covering three acres, the 650-roomed "pretty village" is five stories high in back, stepped down toward a huge plaza that was split down the middle by a wall aligned to true north. The pueblo was repeatedly remodeled, particularly the back section around A.D. 1050, when new rooms and a back wall expanded the size of the entire building. Accessible only from the outside, these new rooms may have functioned as guest quarters and the earlier rooms converted to extra storage during a time of crop shortages.

Subsurface imaging has revealed an extensive network of rooms, kivas, and foundations extending toward nearby Chetro Ketl. This 500-room great house was begun in A.D. 1010 and has a particularly beautiful back wall, the second largest great kiva in the canyon, and two unique features: a raised plaza and a 12th-century Mesoamerican-style colonnade indicating that trade with Mexico (probably for macaws, copper bells, and other sacred objects) also left a mark on the culture.

The planned buildings, large quantities of ceremonial goods, and carefully aligned roads suggest that Chaco's great houses once formed a kind of "Vatican City," inhabited by a few powerful priest-leaders and caretakers, and visited by pilgrims. The priests' in-depth knowledge of astronomy and how it related to the annual planting and ceremonial calendar may have concentrated their power in a society that depended on careful skywatching, obtaining life-giving rain, and predictions for crop success.

A short drought in the 11th century seems to have triggered a flurry of construction activity at Chaco, perhaps to build extra storage space for redistribution of food. But when a long drought cycle set in during the 1100s, the system may finally have broken down, leaving

Tri-walled kiva at Pueblo del Arroyo, sunset. PHOTO ©LARRY ULRICH

Great kiva at Casa Rinconada, early morning. PHOTO ©TOM TILL

Late afternoon at Pueblo Bonito. PHOTO ©JEFF GNASS

The broken walls of Peñasco Blanco, sunset. PHOTO ©SCOTT T. SMITH

Chaco's brilliant leaders with no way of satisfying an increasingly hungry and desperate people who depended on their predictions and who perhaps felt their gods had deserted them.

In the 1100s, the people throughout the region seem to have focused attention on getting by, not constructing masterpieces. Architecture of this late McElmo Phase, as seen at Kin Kletso, Wijiji, and Casa Chiquita, is functional but lacks the finesse and careful planning of earlier times. Existing buildings were often clumsily remodeled, as is evident in the back section of Pueblo Arroyo, which also sports an unusual tri-walled kiva, a style more commonly associated with the northern San Juan area, hinting that newcomers may have moved in for a while. Eventually, everyone left, seeking better-watered farmlands along the Rio Grande, the Puerco Wash, and the Little Colorado River, where their descendants, the modern Pueblo people, live today.

From Albuquerque, it's a 144 mile-drive via US 550 to the park turnoff, just south of Nageezi, then another 21 miles on county roads CR 7900 and CR 7950 (13 miles are dirt), which can become badly washboarded or impassable with rain. Bring food, wood, camping gear, and a full tank of gas—none of these is available in this minimally developed park. Try to arrive by early morning, to avoid intense summertime heat and secure a spot in the small campground.

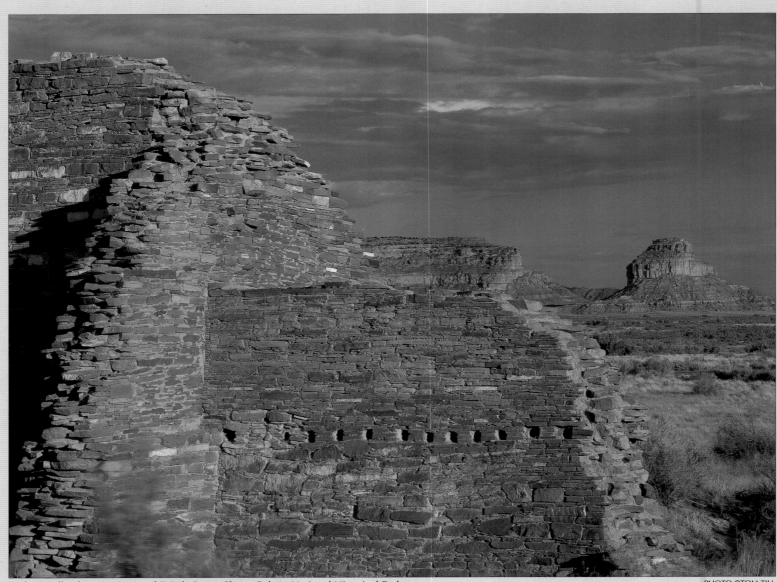

Broken walls of Hungo Pavi and Fajada Butte, Chaco Culture National Historical Park. PHOTO ©TOM TILL

EDGAR LEE HEWETT

Dr. Edgar Lee Hewett was the driving force behind the Antiquities Act of 1906. A modest man with a giant vision, Hewett's "unusual combination of western background, farming and teaching experience, first-hand knowledge of ancient ruins on federal lands in the Southwest, and experience as an archaeologist and administrator" made him, according to historian Ronald Foreman Lee, a force to be reckoned with, able to bring together people across political lines and get things done.

Hewett was born in 1865 in the Midwest. An educator by training, he taught in Colorado, where he met Cora Whitford, a fellow teacher who shared his love of the outdoors. The two were married in September 1891 and spent summer vacations camping in the Rockies. When Cora fell ill with tuberculosis, like many invalids of the time, they moved to New Mexico to recuperate in the warm desert climate. Headquartering in Santa Fe, they spent the summer camping and exploring the Pajarito Plateau, west of the city, which, from then on, became a kind of spiritual retreat for Hewett.

Hewett was named president of the Normal School (now New Mexico Highlands University) in Las Vegas in 1898. He and Cora continued to summer on the Pajarito Plateau, where Edgar carried out an archaeological survey of Ancestral Pueblo sites on the Pajarity Plateau, excavated Frijoles Canyon with the help of students and began lobbying for protection of the whole plateau as a national park. His ideas about co-education, hands-on learning, and proposals for large national parks on western lands caused controversy in traditional New Mexico, and his five-year contract at the school was not renewed.

Hewett learned an important lesson from this setback: build bridges. He went to the University of Geneva and got a Ph.D in anthropology. Then with the backing of eastern academics associated with the American Institute of Archaeology, he excavated at Chaco Canyon, founded the Museum of New Mexico, the School of Archaeology (now the School for Advanced Research), and the anthropology departments at the University of New Mexico and San Diego State University, where he also created the Museum of Man.

In addition to drafting the Antiquities Act that passed in 1906, Hewett is best known for creating Santa Fe Style. With final territorial governor Brad Prince and fellow archaeologist Jesse Nusbaum, he oversaw the restoration of the Palace of the Governors to its original Pueblo Mission style, then worked with architect I. H. Rapp to design the Museum of Fine Arts, Santa Fe's first Santa Fe Style building, in 1917. Hewett died in 1946.

OPPOSITE: The glowing interior walls of Pueblo Bonito, Chaco Culture National Historical Park. PHOTO ©ERIC WUNROW

El Malpais
National Monument

Contorted pines growing on the McCarty Lava Flow. PHOTO ©JEFF GNASS

New Mexico's recent volcanic history can be read in the quiet, eerie landscape preserved since 1987 at 376,000-acre El Malpais National Monument and adjoining El Malpais National Conservation Area in northwestern New Mexico. Beginning two to four million years ago, volcanic eruptions built the 11,300-foot composite volcano Mount Taylor. Then, a million years ago, a series of new volcanoes erupted five different lava flows into this quiet, mesa-encircled valley, south of Grants. The youngest lava flow, the 2,000- to 3,000-year-old McCarty's Flow, is visible alongside Interstate 40, a field of upturned basaltic lava blocks softened here and there with lichens, wildflowers, and trees that have begun to take root.

It's known by its Spanish name, *El Malpais*, "The Badlands," indicating how inhospitable 16th-century Spanish colonists found this terrain as they crossed into New Mexico from New Spain. But to the 100,000 visitors who return to drive the scenic highways and hike and bike each year, El Malpais is a mesmerizing place. It's jointly administered by the National Park Service and Bureau of Land Management and offers wilderness experiences. About 85 percent of the monument is suitable for Congress to designate as wilderness. Within the protected areas are more than 40 volcanoes, numerous spatter vents, lava tubes, and caves.

Sandstone bluffs and Mount Taylor at sunset. PHOTO ©TOM TILL

Stop first at the Northwestern New Mexico Visitor Center in Grants to plan your trip and view the award-winning film "Remembered Earth." There is also a BLM ranger station near the start of NM 117, south of Grants, a good place to begin a drive into El Malpais. A roadside scenic overlook at Sandstone Bluffs has information about the old Garrett Homestead. Northwestern New Mexico was one of the last places in the United States to remain open to homesteading, and this site was built 1935–1937 by homesteaders escaping the Dust Bowl. One of New Mexico's largest natural sandstone arches can be viewed at La Ventana Natural Arch. Near McCarty's Crater, Lava Falls Trail explores the youngest flow in the monument. Picnicking is available at Narrows Picnic Area. There's no campground in El Malpais, but primitive camping is allowed at the picnic area. Bring plenty of water.

County Road 42, also known as Chain of Craters Backcountry Byway for a line of cinder cones, links NM 117 to NM 53. This 36-mile dirt road provides access to backcountry areas in the monument and the Chain of Craters Wilderness Study Area. Hole in the Wall, a backcountry hiking route, leads to a 6,700-acre *kupuka* (island) of ponderosa pine trees surrounded by lava. The 2-mile cairn-marked Big Tubes route crosses a portion of the Bandera lava flow to enter undeveloped lava tubes in the backcountry. There is no light inside; bring three sources of light, including a strong flashlight and extra batteries. An easy 3-mile hiking trail to El Calderon, a 115,000-year-old cinder cone, begins at Milepost 20 on NM 53, three miles north of El Malpais Information Center, which is open daily and has information and a bookstore.

NM 53 begins in the west end of Grants and continues to El Morro National Monument, the Ramah Navajo Reservation, Mormon-founded Ramah, and Zuñi Pueblo, the largest pueblo in New Mexico. The Zuni, Acoma, Laguna, and Ramah Navajo tribes are among the local Indian tribes that continue to use El Malpais, as they have done for centuries. The Zuñi-Acoma Trail, off NM 53, has been an important pueblo trade and ceremonial route for a thousand years. In the late 1940s, Dr. Alfred Dittert excavated a 30–35-room Ancestral Pueblo site off NM 117 that was built between A.D. 1000 and 1300, possibly by people from Chaco Canyon. It is one of more than 60 archaeological sites in Armijo Canyon, and is considered an ancestral site by Acoma Pueblo.

EL MORRO
NATIONAL MONUMENT

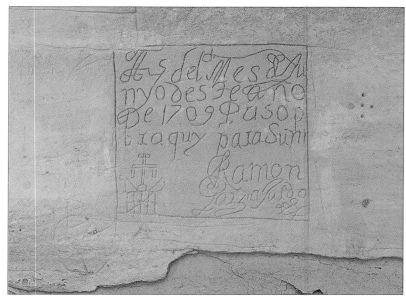

Inscription left by Ramon Garcia Jurado in 1709. PHOTO ©TOM DANIELSEN

For 700 years, travelers through the high desert of northwestern New Mexico were drawn to a 230-foot-high sandstone monolith called El Morro to drink from a permanent protected pool of water at the base of the sheer cliffs. Until the building of the railroad, to the north, put it out of business, El Morro was the most important water source for 30 miles. What draws visitors today, however, are the inscriptions in the soft, creamy Zuni Sandstone carved by Ancestral Pueblo people, Spanish explorers and settlers, and American emigrants. Some 2,000-odd inscriptions and petroglyphs cover the base of El Morro, forming a unique visual record of New Mexico's colorful early history.

The Ancestral Pueblo people who were the earliest known users of El Morro farmed the region and lived in stone villages, or pueblos, built around a central plaza. It may have been severe drought and the need to defend scarce resources that led people to build 875-room Atsinna Pueblo atop the sandstone bluff in A.D. 1275. They remained at Atsinna (translated as Where Pictures Are on the Rock) for a couple of generations, then moved on, perhaps looking for lands with longer growing seasons than this 7,000-foot elevation allowed and less exposed to the elements. They carved bighorn sheep, bear claws, anthropomorphs, handprints, and zigzag lines, concentric circles, and other geometric symbols into the cliff. Although cryptic to us today, these inscriptions continue to have meaning to their descendants, the Zuni, who travel to El Morro from their adjoining reservation for ceremonies and plant gathering.

The inhabitants of Zuni Pueblo were the first people encountered by 16th-century Spanish conquistadors traveling into New Mexico in search of fabled wealth—a clash of cultures that would change Pueblo lives forever. In the century that followed, two important names in Spanish history—first New Mexico governor Don Juan de Oñate, in 1602, and Don Diego de Vargas, hero of the Reconquest in 1692—camped here enroute to headquarters in Santa Fe. De Vargas was the first to refer to the bluff as *El Morro* in 1692. Using the favored *Paso Por Aqui*—"Passed by here"—numerous Spaniards used the rock face to commemorate their exploits, from new discoveries and peace missions to avenging the death of missionary priests martyred by Indians.

The first Europeans to record the petroglyphs on Inscription Rock, as it came to be called, were U.S. Army Lt. J. H. Simpson and artist R. H. Kern, who were led here by a Navajo Indian in September 1849,

Petroglyphs at Inscription Rock. PHOTO ©LAURENCE PARENT

during a survey of Southwest lands ceded to the United States following the U.S.–Mexico War. Changes came upon the Southwest with the speed of a juggernaut, as Americans moved onto western lands. Several beautifully rendered inscriptions were made on August 23, 1857, by Lt. Edward Beale and P. Gilmer Breckinridge, who was acting as a camel wrangler for 25 camels being tested as pack animals on an expedition to blaze a route from Texas to California. The first American emigrant wagon train to use the Santa Fe Trail stopped at El Morro on July 7 and 8, 1858, and left 26 names. Some of the last historic inscriptions on the rocks were made by a Union Pacific Railroad crew surveying the Zuni-Acoma Trail for a new railroad in 1868. A distinctive "U.P.R." appends their names.

El Morro's significant role in early New Mexico history led it to be designated New Mexico's first national monument under the new Antiquities Act of 1906. The monument is 43 miles from Grants, along NM 53, and open daily. It has two easy trails: half-mile Inscription Trail around the base of the rock, and two-mile Mesa Top Trail, which includes the inscription loop and then a more strenuous hike to Atsinna Pueblo. A nine-site primitive campground has water for a fee, May–October; dry camping is free the rest of the year.

OPPOSITE: Atsinna Pueblo atop El Morro, sunset. PHOTO ©GEORGE H.H. HUEY

FORT UNION
NATIONAL MONUMENT

Remains of the Officer's Quarters. PHOTO ©LAURENCE PARENT

Its lonely adobe buildings are now melting into the earth, and little remains to indicate that the ruins of the mid-19th-century fort on the western edge of this windswept valley in northeastern New Mexico was once one of the largest and most important frontier forts in the Southwest. Over a 40-year period, three forts were built here to serve travelers on the 900-mile-long Santa Fe Trail, which opened in 1821 from Missouri to New Mexico. Traders, supply wagons, mail stages, and settlers who had for years braved heat, dust, lack of water, plagues of insects, illness, and Indian depredations to reach Santa Fe could complete their journey under army escort, after many anxious weeks on the trail.

The first fort, built by Colonel Edwin Sumner and his men in 1851, was a small log-and-earth garrison and supply depot, which was hot, buggy, and hard to maintain. It was built strategically close to the junction of the Mountain and Cimarron Cutoff branches of the Santa Fe Trail, just after the Southwest became U.S. territory, so that soldiers could protect new U.S. citizens—Hispanic and Anglo—from Jicarilla Apaches, Kiowas, Utes, and Comanches who frequented the area.

This first Fort Union was abandoned in 1861, when a number of Fort Union's officers left to join the Confederacy, and New Mexico, which briefly yielded to the Confederates in the southern part of the state, faced a major confrontation with the Texas Confederates for control of the New Mexico Territory and Colorado goldfields. A new commander, Colonel Edward R.S. Canby, supplemented the few remaining soldiers with a battalion of Colorado Volunteers and built a star-shaped, semi–subterranean earthworks fort in preparation for a battle. In the end, the Colorado Volunteers, along with regular troops and New Mexico Volunteer units, fought the key western battle in the Civil War near the Rio Grande, at Glorieta Pass, in what is now part of Pecos National Historical Park. New Mexico was saved for the Union when the soldiers found and destroyed the Confederate supply wagons, forcing the Confederates to retreat.

The final fort was built between 1863 and 1869 to serve as the central supply post for the western armed forces and as a base of operations against Indian incursions that continued until 1875. The new fort cost a million dollars and was built of limewashed adobe, with porticoed homes for the officers. It had a military post, a big quartermaster's depot and warehouses, the largest hospital in the area, a jail, corrals, workshops, offices, quarters, a parade ground, and a sutler store. By the 1870s, officers,

Cannon on the Parade Ground. PHOTO ©LAURENCE PARENT

enlisted men, families, and civilian workers lived at the fort. With army assistance, westward expansion, trade, and communication began to boom.

When the railroad extended to nearby Las Vegas, New Mexico in 1879, the fort began to decline due to decreased traffic on the Santa Fe Trail. It was finally abandoned in 1891. In 1956, Fort Union was set aside as a national monument. The Santa Fe Trail was designated a national historic trail in 1987. Today, at the 720-acre monument, visitors can see the ruins of the third fort, the imprints of the first two forts, and deep wagon ruts of the Santa Fe Trail. A self-guided trail with push-button audio vignettes tours the ruins of the final fort. Fort Union is particularly lively on summer weekends, when costumed living-history interpreters are stationed in the grounds. The visitor center is open daily and has information, exhibits, an audiovisual program, and a bookstore. Picnicking is allowed but there is no camping; the nearest developed campground is at Storrie Lake State Park, five miles northwest of Las Vegas.

OPPOSITE: Late afternoon at the Mechanic's Corral. PHOTO ©LAURENCE PARENT

GILA CLIFF
DWELLINGS NATIONAL MONUMENT

Prickly pear cactus and dwelling tucked into cliff alcove. PHOTO ©TOM DANIELSEN

High in the cliffs above the Gila River in southwest New Mexico sits a small stone village tucked into a series of alcoves, as silent as the seven centuries that have slipped away since its construction. The Gila Cliff Dwellings were built during a severe drought between the 1270s and 1290s by late-Tularosa Phase Mogollon from the Reserve area, 50 miles to the northwest. Between 40 and 60 people lived in this 42-room pueblo for just a generation before moving on about A.D.1300. Gila Cliff Dwellings National Monument was set aside in 1907 to preserve the dwellings as the best representation of Mogollon remains in the region. It is the only Mogollon site within the National Park System.

The Mogollon were the Southwest's first cultural innovators. Around 200 B.C., they began making beautiful red-brown pottery and farming corn—techniques learned from their Mexican neighbors. But so bountiful was the Gila high country, they continued to hunt and gather. Mule deer, bison, and elk provided meat and fat, hides for clothing, and bones for tools. Small rodents, such as pocket gophers, squirrels, and rabbits, were daily fare, along with trout and other coldwater fish caught in clear streams. And quantities of pinyon nuts, walnuts, and acorns, yucca, pricklypear, wild grapes, and other food, medicine, and utilitarian plants grew here.

The Mogollon were mountain people, content to live in snug pithouses for 1,000 years. Eventually, though, they moved from hamlets on hilltops to valley-bottom locations near fields, where their numbers grew and they began to trade and live in stone villages. Mogollon culture reached its aesthetic zenith between A.D. 1000 and 1150 with the Mimbres Mogollon, who farmed the nearby Mimbres River Valley. The Mimbres lived on a busy trade route between Casas Grandes, Mexico, and Chaco Canyon and bartered their woven cotton, pinyon nuts, and stunning black-on-white pottery decorated with unique geometric and animal scenes for young scarlet macaws, copper bells, shell bracelets, turquoise, and other exotica.

The Tularosa Mogollon came to Cliff Dweller Canyon in the late 1270s and built single and multistory dwellings, constructed from local ponderosa pine beams and rough masonry of Gila Conglomerate rock laid in mud mortar. Walls and a few roofs complemented the natural cooling and heating advantages provided by the caves and alcoves. Small vents facing the canyon may have served as smoke exits, light entries, or spy holes. Within and around these walls, women ground corn, cooked, made pottery, and cared for children in small plazas. Rectangular kivas provided sacred spaces for communal activities. The men hunted game using bows and arrows, traps and snares, and used ladders, stone niche steps, and game trails to travel between the dwellings and their fields along the river and the mesa tops.

Today a one-mile, self-guided trail with a 180-foot elevation gain leads through Cliff Dweller Canyon to the six caves and back to a parking area and trailhead contact station. The dwellings are open from 8 a.m. to 6 p.m. in summer (9 a.m. to 4 p.m. the rest of the year). Rangers lead tours at 11 a.m. and 2 p.m. daily in summer (noon only in winter). Bring food and bottled water—the monument has neither—and wear a hat and sunscreen. The Gila Visitor Center, located two miles from the trailhead, is open daily except for major holidays and has exhibits, a bookstore, and information on hiking and camping in the adjoining USFS Gila Wilderness.

Gila Cliff Dwellings is 44 miles north of Silver City via NM 15, a narrow, winding, paved road that takes two hours to drive (RVs should use NM 35). NM 15 and adjoining NM 35 form part of the Trail of the Mountain Spirits National Scenic Byway. Attractions include Gila Hot Springs, Lake Roberts, Pinos Altos, Buffalo Soldiers exhibits at Fort Bayard, the Southwestern New Mexico Birding Trail, and the 3.3-million-acre Gila National Forest and Gila Wilderness, designated in 1924 as the nation's first wilderness.

OPPOSITE: Gila Cliff Dwellings. PHOTO ©KERRICK JAMES

Pecos
NATIONAL HISTORICAL PARK

Kiva (in foreground with ladder) and church. PHOTO ©EDUARDO FUSS

Pecos Pueblo, or *Cicuye*, is no longer recognizable for the might city-state it was in the 1500s. But when Spanish conquistador Coronado saw it in 1540, it wielded unimaginable power as a trading center from its fortress setting on a small mesa halfway between the Great Plains and the Rio Grande. Cicuye came to dominate this forested mountain basin between the Sangre de Cristo Mountains and Glorieta Mesa, 25 miles east of Santa Fe, in the 1300s. At that time, smaller pueblos were coalescing into large, defensible cities, as populations along the Rio Grande swelled with newcomers arriving from drought-ridden Four Corners locations. The growing season in the chilly, 7,000-foot-elevation Pecos Valley was short, and settlement had always been sparse. Pecos had to buy and sell most of what it required and used its location on a cultural frontier to full advantage, becoming a powerful trade center.

It's a measure of the success of the Spanish colonists that they did, in fact, subdue indomitable Pecos Pueblo. The confident leaders had welcomed Coronado at Zuñi in 1540, and would do so again, when the first Spanish colonial governor, Don Juan de Oñate, arrived in 1598. Things changed when Franciscan missionaries built a chapel outside the pueblo in 1617, followed, in 1620–1625, by 6,000-square-foot Nuestra Señora de los Angeles de Porciuncula mission church, built by Padre Andres Juarez. The new church was the largest church in New Mexico. It had 55-foot-high, whitewashed walls of 300,000 adobe bricks, six belltowers, beautifully carved beams, and huge buttresses. Next door was a *convento*, or living, teaching, and working quarters, and *estancia*, or small farm, where Spanish sheep and cattle were corraled with chickens.

The Pueblo world began to fall apart, riven by disagreements and caught between the conflicting demands of Spanish settlers and Pueblo leaders. The church at Pecos was burned in 1680, during the Pueblo Revolt. A smaller church was built following the Reconquest of 1692, reflecting an Indian population decimated by disease, famine, and Comanche raids. The Comanche signed a peace treaty at Pecos in 1786, clearing the way for Spanish settlement of the Pecos Valley. San Miguel de Vado quickly usurped Pecos's role as a trading center, and settlers in the Pecos River Canyon took Pecos Pueblo land.

In 1838, the remaining Pecos residents walked 80 miles to Jemez Pueblo to join their Towa-speaking relatives. They left behind a painting in the church in the nearby Hispanic village of Pecos that had once hung in the mission church. Today, the painting is the centerpiece of an annual August feast day procession to the park, where, in 1999, the remains of 2,000 Pecos descendants were returned for reburial.

Pecos became a national historical park in 1990 after a long campaign by Texas oilman E. E. "Buddy" Fogelson and his wife, actress Greer Garson. The couple owned 13,000-acre Forked Lightning Ranch, which included the Forked Lightning Ranch House, designed by Santa Fe architect John Gaw Meem in 1926. Pecos National Historical Park also now encompassed two locations of the 1862 Battle of Glorieta Pass that changed the course of the Civil War in the West; Kozlowski's Trading Post, a popular spot on the Santa Fe Trail in the mid-1800s; and 12th-century Forked Lightning Pueblo, excavated by A. V. Kidder between 1915 and 1929.

Kidder's work at Pecos profoundly influenced Southwest archaeology: the Pecos classification system of dating historic periods using ceramics is the gold standard today. Some 80,000 extraordinary artifacts are displayed in the visitor center, from which you can tour the pueblo and church on the 1.5-mile self-guided ruins trail. Special tours of Civil War sites, Forked Lightning Ranch and Pueblo, and Santa Fe Trail ruts are offered in summer (weekends the rest of the year). The park also has demonstrations of carving, breadmaking, pottery, basketry, and other trades at the E.E. Fogelson Visitor Center in summer.

OPPOSITE: Arched doorway in the mission church. PHOTO ©EDUARDO FUSS

Petroglyphs at dawn. PHOTO ©TOM TILL

PETROGLYPH
NATIONAL MONUMENT

Petroglyph National Monument protects the ancient petroglyphs carved into the 17-mile-long volcanic escarpment of West Mesa, west of the Rio Grande within the City of Albuquerque. With 20,000 recorded petroglyphs, the national monument preserves one of the most impressive collections of Indian and Hispanic rock inscriptions in the world. In addition, more than 350 archaeological sites and a variety of volcanic features associated with the Rio Grande Rift Zone and accompanying wildlife habitats can be found in the 11-square-mile monument.

Most of these Rio Grande–style petroglyphs were created by Ancestral Pueblo people between A.D. 1300 and 1650, a period when contact with Europeans marked the transition from prehistoric to historic times. Newcomers fleeing the Four Corners drought arrived in the 1300s, sparking many cultural advances. The unexcavated Piedras Marcadas pueblo site on the northeast side of the monument, with more than 1,000 rooms on the ground floor alone, was one of many large pueblos built to accommodate the newcomers. At the base of the escarpment, remnant field houses and water control features made of basalt signal crop cultivation. Seasonal crops were supplemented with ricegrass seeds and many other wild foods that grew along the mesa top, as well as mule deer and rabbits that inhabit the zone between the mesa and floodplain.

The dramatic inscriptions here include the familiar humpbacked flute player known as Kokopelli, reptiles, birds, insects, and four-legged animals, anthropomorphs, geometric designs, and mysterious masked serpents and star beings. Some may be 2,000 to 3,000 years old, dating back to the dawn of Basketmaker culture, when people still lived in pithouses. The symbols were probably used in ceremonies: modern Pueblo people consider the area an open-air church and make pilgrimages to perform ceremonies here.

When New Mexico became Spanish territory, heirs of the Atrisco Land Grant given to settlers by the Spanish Crown visited the petroglyphs and carved crosses and sheep brands into the 150,000-year-old basaltic rock. Later, during the 1800s, ranchers pecked their names and dates into the dark surfaces of the boulders. In the late 20th century, repeated vandalism of the petroglyphs sparked concern among local people, who lobbied hard for protection. Indian Petroglyph State Park and Volcano Park were set aside in the 1970s, but only with designation as a national monument in 1990 was full federal preservation given to an expanded area. Burgeoning growth on the west side of Albuquerque abutting the monument continually challenges managers to protect the resources. But locals continue to fight hard on behalf of their monument, and some 150,000 visitors a year come to hike and marvel at this backyard treasure.

Stop first at the visitor center on Unser Boulevard, which has information, exhibits, and lectures, demonstrations, and other programs on summer weekends. Boca Negra, formerly Indian Petroglyph State Park, is three miles north of the visitor center and has three partially paved trails, water, toilets, and picnic tables managed by the City of Albuquerque. The park service manages three undeveloped units: Rinconada Canyon, one mile south of the visitor center, which has a 2.5 mile round-trip unpaved trail to the base of the escarpment; Piedras Marcadas, accessed via a small parking lot west of Golf Course Road, off Montano Road; and the Volcanoes section, off Paseo de Volcan, where you can view five small volcanoes and geologic windows from hiking trails. Toilets are available but no water; dogs are allowed on a leash, except at Boca Negra Canyon. To reach the monument from the south, take exit 155 for Unser Boulevard and exit 149 for Paseo de Volcan from westbound Interstate 40. From the north, Paradise Road leads to Unser and Volcano from Interstate 25 through Rio Rancho to Double Eagle Airport. The 5,000-foot-elevation monument is very exposed. Bring plenty of water, wear a hat, sunscreen, and strong footwear. Watch out for rattlesnakes.

OPPOSITE: "Lion" petroglyph, Rinconada Canyon. PHOTO ©GEORGE H.H. HUEY

SALINAS PUEBLO
MISSIONS NATIONAL MONUMENT

Church walls at Abó. PHOTO ©LAURENCE PARENT

Salinas Pueblo Missions National Monument, located amid the sweeping grasslands of central New Mexico's Estancia Basin, preserves three of the oldest 17th-century Spanish mission ruins in the United States. Gran Quivira received federal protection in 1909; the former state monuments of Abó and Quarai were added to form the new Salinas National Monument in 1980. It was later renamed Salinas Pueblo Missions National Monument. Although these peaceful, ruined pueblo missions appear similar at first glance, as you study the Pueblo and Spanish architecture and learn about the political upheavals and natural disasters that shook Spanish New Mexico, you soon realize that Abó, Quarai, and Gran Quivira have unique stories to tell.

Long before humans began living in New Mexico, a warm shallow tropical sea dominated the Estancia Basin. A drying trend caused the sea to shrink and be replaced by a large lake, which attracted Pleistocene big game, such as mammoth and bison, as well as paleo-hunters who followed the herds into the Southwest at the end of the last ice age. As the climate heated up, the lake evaporated altogether, leaving behind large salt beds, or *salinas*. This salt became a prized trade item for prehistoric people and a commodity the Spanish would come to call "one of New Mexico's four treasures."

Around A.D. 900, small family groups were farming in the Estancia Basin, using runoff from mountain highlands and natural springs at Abó and Quarai to irrigate their crops. By the 12th century, *jacal* (wattle-and-daub) structures and pithouse dwellings had evolved into *pueblos*, or masonry villages. The absence of springs at Gran Quivira meant that water had to be collected in cisterns. Marginal living at Gran Quivira led to this southernmost pueblo in New Mexico having to rely heavily on trade by the 1400s. The pueblo lay on a trading hub between the Rio Grande pueblos to the north, the Plains Indians to the east, the Pacific cultures to the west, and the Mesoamerican cultures to the south. Early Spanish visitors dubbed the thriving community Pueblo de Las Humanas, in reference to the many people with stripe-painted faces living at the pueblo. The name Gran Quivira eventually took hold in the 19th century, given that name by Americans from the East who began settling the area.

Abó and Quarai were strategically located between western and northern pueblos and the Estancia Basin, giving them a trade advantage, also. By the time Spanish settlers arrived in 1598, the region was a bustling melting pot of native cultures that bartered animal products, pottery, precious stones, feathers, piñon nuts, and corn.

Around 1622, the pueblo of Abó (along with some other pueblos in the region) took an oath of allegiance to the Spanish Act of Obedience, which allowed Fray (Father) Francisco Fonte to begin a Catholic mission there. Four years later, the pueblo of Quarai followed suit, under the direction of Fray Juan Gutierrez de la Chica. Pueblo de Las Humanas was the last to take the oath. In 1629, Las Humanas was visited by Fray Alonso Benavides, the new *custos* (custodian), whose arrival in New Mexico in 1626 sped up the missionary efforts in the Salinas Province.

Abó and Quarai are typical missions of the period, with their red sandstone churches and *conventos* featuring *porterias* (waiting rooms), patios, *ambulatorios* (walkways), monk's cells, kitchens, and storage rooms. Abó also administered the *visitas* (satellite missions) of neighboring Tenabó and the southern mission of Las Humanas, now known as Gran Quivira. As a mark of its prosperity, the small church of San Gregorio de Abó was replaced by a larger church in 1651. Like Quarai, it is a fine example of frontier architecture with high tapering walls, a long nave, transepts, a baptistry, sacristy, and choir loft. It also featured a clerestory window, which illuminated the altar to maximum effect using natural light.

At Gran Quivira, around 1630, Fray Francisco Letrado directed construction of the church and convento of San Isidro using local limestone. Gran Quivira was a visita of Abó until the arrival, in 1659, of Fray Diego de Santander at the remote pueblo who began construction of a new church and convento named for San Buenaventura.

The Spanish system of *encomienda*, allowing Spanish lords to collect grain and other commodities from Pueblos in return for assisting the crown in assimilating these indigenous peoples, pitted government against Franciscan. Inquiries by the Spanish Inquisition, whose representatives were quartered at Quarai, further split friars, officials, and *encomenderos*, with the Pueblos caught in the middle.

Friction caused by the Spanish encomienda system was exacerbated by a long drought in the 1660s, accompanied by a severe famine. The situation was further aggravated by Apache raids. By the time the

The walls of Quarai. PHOTO ©KERRICK JAMES

Church walls at Quarai. PHOTO ©TOM DANIELSEN

Sunrise at Gran Quivira. PHOTO ©WILLARD CLAY

Rainbow above the church at Abó. PHOTO ©GEORGE H.H. HUEY

Pueblo Revolt erupted in 1680, the southern pueblo missions lay empty, many of their inhabitants left dead from starvation, and the survivors dispersed to the pueblos of the middle Rio Grande, whose languages and cultures were similar.

To reach Abó, drive south from Albuquerque on Interstate 25 to Belen, turning east on US 60. Abó is nine miles west of Mountainair. To reach Quarai, drive east on Interstate 40 to Tijeras and drop down on NM 337, a pretty route known as the Salt Trail. Quarai is eight miles north of Mountainair just off NM 55 at Punta de Agua. To reach Gran Quivira, take NM 55 south of Mountainair and drive another 26 miles. Each mission has a staffed visitor center, exhibits, a bookstore, and a self-guided trail with wayside signs telling the story of the pueblos and their missions. Gas, food, and lodging are available in the tiny ranching community of Mountainair, where park headquarters for the national monument can be found. The friendly visitor center, on the south side of US Hwy 60, offers exhibits and a film telling the story of all three missions, as well as a bookstore. It is highly recommended as a starting point for your visit. The monument is open daily from 9 a.m. to 5 p.m.

White Sands
National Monument

Pre-dawn light illuminates Heart of the Sands. PHOTO ©LARRY ULRICH

It comes into view like a bizarre desert mirage, 15 miles southwest of Alamogordo, in southern New Mexico: 275 square miles of the world's largest gypsum dunes, 40 percent of which are preserved in White Sands National Monument. Constantly changing form, ebbing and flowing, buffeted by blowing winds, the dunes undulate across the Tularosa Basin, New Mexico's Space Central, a fitting place for such an alien landscape.

Actually, the origins of this strange sight are quite earthly, and close by. Gypsum, a hydrous form of calcium sulfate, was originally deposited at the bottom of the ancient Permian Sea, which became landlocked and evaporated here, 250 million years ago. The sedimentary layers later domed up, then, about 10 million years ago, the center collapsed, creating the San Andres Mountains to the west and the Sacramento Mountains to the east. Gypsum is washed down into the basin from the ranges, where the runoff is trapped in low-lying ephemeral lakes that evaporate in the sizzling heat of the Chihuahuan Desert. The resulting daggerlike gypsum crystals are blasted apart by extreme temperatures and southwesterly winds that sweep across the valley in springtime.

Strong winds bounce sand-sized gypsum grains along the ground, where they form dunes of different sizes and shapes that, in turn, affect further deposition. Dunes are stabilized by subsurface mineral crystallization, but despite apparent immobility, their shapes change constantly. At the eastern edge of the dune field are crescent-shaped parabolic dunes, slowest-moving of the dunes due to weaker winds blowing across their surface and stabilizing hardy desert plants that tolerate the alkaline environment, such as four-wing saltbush, iodinebush, and soaptree yucca. Barchan dunes are also crescent shaped but their "arms" point downwind, ahead of the dunes. Barchan dunes can reach 65 feet high and are found in the center of the dune field, along with transverse dunes, which form long, undulating ridges like a series of waves at sea.

It's extraordinary how many desert animals live among these dunes, adapting themselves to the particular demands of the environment. Kangaroo rats, whose physiology allows them to recycle all the water they need from seeds, burrow beneath the dunes to stay cool. Mice and lizards adopt a white camouflage to blend with the snowy background. Western diamondback and desert massasauga rattlesnakes lie motionless in the shade when it heats up and become active at sunset when temperatures cool, along with kit foxes, coyotes, and other nocturnal rodent-hunters. Finches, doves, thrashers, and shrikes are among the birds that can be seen from the Dune Life Nature Trail and Boardwalk Trail. A 4.5-mile loop into the heart of the dunes, Alkali Flat Trail, leaves from the end of the Dunes Drive.

The monument's youngest dunes are found in the southwest corner of the monument near Lake Lucero, where winds are strongest. They are dome-shaped frontier dunes, which migrate some 30 feet a year, making them the most active dunes in the basin. The fast-moving sand allows few plants to grow here. Due to their proximity to White Sands Missile Range (site of the first atomic bomb test in 1945), the dome-shaped dunes may not be seen by visitors. Three-hour ranger-led tours to the west edge of Lake Lucero to see the gypsum crystal beds are available monthly by advance reservation.

With over 450,000 visitors a year—many of them local, drawn from adjoining Holloman Air Force Base and nearby Las Cruces and Alamogordo—White Sands is the most visited unit of the National Park System in New Mexico. The entrance to the popular 16-mile Dune Drive loop opens at 7 a.m. and closes at 9 p.m. in the summer: visitors have to be out of the park by 10 p.m. On Full Moon nights, the entrance closes at 10 p.m. and visitors need to be out by 11 p.m. The Dunes Drive is periodically closed for periods of up to three hours due to testing on the adjacent White Sands Missile Range. The Dunes Drive closes at sunset in winter: visitors must leave by one hour after sunset. In addition to the trails, there is a popular picnic area with picnic tables shaded by unusual curving sun shelters designed by Lyle Bennett in the 1930s. Bennett also designed White Sands Visitor Center, which, along with seven other adjacent Pueblo Revival–style buildings built between 1936 and 1940 as part of the statewide Works Progress Administration, was officially designated White Sands National Monument Historic District in 1990.

Monument commemorating the world's first atomic bomb test at Trinity Site

THE BOMB

"Everybody who goes there will go crazy." So predicted physicist Leo Szilard, referring to the remote location of Los Alamos ("the cottonwoods"), on the Pajarito Plateau, where scientists raced to split the atom and build America's first bombs during World War II. The site chosen by lead scientist J. Robert Oppenheimer and U.S. Army General Leslie Groves in November 1942 was the former Los Alamos Ranch School, built in 1917 for wealthy boys to receive a balanced education that included both rigorous academics and outdoor experiences.

For the next three years, "Site Y," as it was known, was home to many of the world's top scientists. They included big-name physicists and theoreticians like Denmark's Niels Bohr and England's Sir James Chadwick, both of whom had worked with Rutherford, the English nuclear pioneer; Italians Enrico Fermi and Emilio Segre; Hungarian-born Edward Teller, who went on to father the hydrogen bomb (the superbomb); Otto Frisch, who coined the term "fission"; and Americans Luis Alvarez and Richard Feynman.

With victory achieved in Europe by May 1945, America focused on ending the war in the Pacific by dropping a bomb on the Japanese mainland. A site in the desert of southern New Mexico, known appropriately as the Jornada del Muerto (Dead Man's Way) and dubbed Trinity Site by Oppenheimer—was selected to test the bomb on Monday, July 16, 1945. Successfully detonated at 5:30 a.m., it evaporated the steel tower

that held it, created a 25-foot-deep crater, and caused an explosion heard 50 miles away and a huge flash visible for more than 250 miles. The megablast's impact was equivalent to some 18,000 tons of TNT, and deadly radiation was unleashed over an area of about a hundred miles. Shaken by the implications of what had occurred, Oppenheimer intoned the following words from the classic Hindu devotional poem *Bhagavad Gita*: "I am become Death, the shatterer of Worlds."

On August 6, 1945, the uranium bomb dubbed "Little Boy" was dropped from the *Enola Gay* at 9:15 a.m., leveling Hiroshima and killing 130,000 men, women, and children. The plutonium bomb nicknamed "Fat Man" came next, devastating Nagasaki three days later, killing 75,000 people, and ending the war in the Pacific. Today, Los Alamos National Laboratory continues to be controversial, applying science and technology in strategies involving national security. It also works with the private sector to create new technologies, such as the explosive used to inflate air bags in cars.

Trinity Site is located on White Sands Missile Range near Alamogordo. You can visit this national historical landmark on the first day of April and October with military escort. Tours begin at 8 a.m. and return at 3 p.m. Call (575) 437-6120 or toll-free (800) 826-0294 for details. Museums about New Mexico's atomic program are located in Los Alamos and Albuquerque.

OPPOSITE: Soaptree yuccas in Heart of The Dunes. PHOTO ©JEFF GNASS

BEYOND THE NATIONAL PARKS

White pelicans at Bosque del Apache National Wildlife Refuge. PHOTO ©TIM FITZHARRIS

While New Mexico's 13 national parks are a highlight of a visit to the Land of Enchantment, the state also offers an extraordinary array of city, county, and state parks and museums as well as sites managed by other federal land management agencies such as the BLM and Indian tribes. These units offer a deeper look at the state's diverse natural and cultural history, and many provide added recreational opportunities not available at national parks. Many of New Mexico's 34 state parks, for example, protect lakes and provide much-needed swimming, boating, and fishing opportunities on the water—a commodity in short supply in this desert state. Similarly, the state's national forests offer an opportunity to travel into cool, forested mountains to escape summer heat and snowshoe in winter. The Museum of New Mexico's five Santa Fe museums and six state monuments each add to an understanding of New Mexico's fascinating tricultural history. Different use rules and fees apply to each of the 17 selected destinations below. Contact each unit for information. Some destinations, such as the spectacular new Valles Caldera National Preserve in the Jemez Mountains, only allow entry by special use permit; reservations must be made in advance but the rewards will be great—few people have had chance to visit this incredible backcountry treasure yet. Other destinations, such as the BLM-run Kasha-Katuwe Tent Rocks National Monument, collect admission fees on the honor system and their entire budget comes from onsite use fees. Kasha-Katuwe is located on Indian land. As always, when visiting Indian Country, enjoy yourself but please be respectful and stay in authorized areas. You are traveling across sovereign nations within the United States. It's a privilege, not a right.

BISTI BADLANDS

The Bisti/De-Na-Zin Wilderness encompasses 45,000 acres of remote badlands, 20 miles south of Farmington, off NM 371. It was set aside in 1996 to protect its important record of changes in plant and animal life at the end of the Age of Dinosaurs, 65 million years ago. The Fruitland Formation and Kirtland Shale formed in coastal swamps and contain sandstone, shale, mudstone, coal, and silt that have been eroded into spires, toadstool-shaped hoodoos, and crumbly hills scorched red by ancient subterranean coal fires. Numerous fossils have been found, including duck-billed dinosaurs and petrified wood. Administered by the

BLM, the Bisti (Bis-**tie**) and De-Na-Zin (named for nearby petroglyphs of cranes) have no services and can only be entered on foot. Bring food, water, sun protection, and let someone know where you are. Several dirt county roads (impassable after rain) lead from the wilderness to Chaco Culture National Historical Park. For information, call (505) 599-8900 or log on to www.nm.blm.gov.

BOSQUE DEL APACHE NATIONAL WILDLIFE REFUGE

Some 300 bird species are attracted to this expansive area of marshes, ponds, farmland, and riparian forest on a bend in the Rio Grande, near Socorro, some 90 miles south of Albuquerque. But it's not the number of species that attracts birding enthusiasts; it's the sheer number of birds that congregate here. Tens of thousands of snow geese, ducks, and sandhill cranes arrive in winter, along with bald and golden eagles, kestrels, and northern harriers. Birdwatchers come from around the world to view and photograph the spine-chilling sunrise and sunset takeoffs of these migratory waterfowl from *bosques* (bottomlands) along the Rio Grande. A schedule of nature walks and workshops is offered year round. The annual Festival of Cranes, held the weekend before Thanksgiving, is the highlight of the year. For information, call (505) 835-1828 or log on to www.friendsofthebosque.org.

CAMINO REAL DE TIERRA ADENTRO NATIONAL HISTORICAL TRAIL

This national historic trail extends 404 miles from El Paso, Texas, to San Juan Pueblo, New Mexico and commemorates the primary route used for 300 years by travelers between Mexico City and provincial capitals in New Mexico. Every three years, colonial administrators used this route to send important supplies north to missions in New Mexico, which then sent back local goods such as Pueblo-woven cloth (*mantas*), Navajo wool rugs, Estancia Basin salt, and captive Apache laborers. El Camino Real International Heritage Center, 30 miles south of Socorro, interprets El Camino Real (the Royal Road) with exhibits and special events. It is part of the 28-mile scenic byway along Highway 1, between San Antonio and Exit 115, that includes Fort Craig, an important Civil War site, and Bosque del Apache National Wildlife Refuge. For information, call (505) 988-6888 or log on to www.elcaminoreal.org.

Exotic rock formations, Bisti Badlands. PHOTO ©TOM DANIELSEN

Kiva and Sandia Mountains, Coronado State Monument. PHOTO ©LAURENCE PARENT

CITY OF ROCKS STATE PARK
City of Rocks is off US 180, between Silver City and Deming in southwestern New Mexico's "bootheel." Composed of volcanic tuff deposited more than 30 million years ago and subsequently exposed by erosion, stone knobs some 40 feet tall stand like thumbs in the torrid flats of the Chihuahuan Desert. It's said that the outlaw Billy the Kid—who spent his youth in Silver City—hid among these formations. A gravel road loops around the park, but most people like to walk through the labyrinthine passageways. City of Rocks is best visited when temperatures are cooler. There is a very pleasant campground here. Funky Faywood Hot Springs is located next door. For information, call (575) 536-2800 or log on to www.emnrd.state.nm.us.

CORONADO STATE MONUMENT
This state monument commemorates the site of the Tiwa-speaking pueblo of Kuaua, one of a dozen towns in the province of Tiguex, a 30-mile corridor flanking the Rio Grande. Although no hard evidence has been found, historians believe that its leaders may have offered the entire pueblo of Kuaua to Coronado and his men as winter quarters in 1540, after news of their conquest of Zuni Pueblo spread north. Founded in A.D. 1300, Kauau grew into a 1,200-room fortress at the crossroads between the Ancestral Pueblo and Mogollon cultures. An excellent self-guided trail circles what remains of the ruined pueblo, with stops at capped adobe walls and reconstructed kivas that show both Mogollon and Ancestral Pueblo influences. A small museum offers an overview of the Indian and Hispanic history of the area. A separate building houses mysterious ceremonial kachina murals, which were removed for safekeeping from the great kiva following excavations by the Civilian Conservation Corps during the 400th anniversary of Coronado's arrival. For information, call (505) 867-5351 or log on to www.nmmonuments.org.

CUMBRES and TOLTEC SCENIC RAILROAD
The historic Cumbres & Toltec Scenic Railroad is a 64-mile, narrow gauge steam railroad jointly owned by the states of New Mexico and Colorado. It was constructed in 1880 as part of the Rio Grande's San Juan Extension, which served the silver mining district of the San Juan Mountains in southwestern Colorado. But unlike other sections of the Rio Grande, it was never converted to the standard four feet and 8.5 inches track in 1890. The railroad subsequently languished until the track and line-side structures, nine steam locomotives, over 130 freight and work cars, and the Chama yard and maintenance facility were purchased for use as a tourist train in 1970. Operational between May 27 and October 15, the Cumbres & Toltec runs seven days a week between the towns of Chama, New Mexico, and Antonito, Colorado, stopping for hot or boxed lunch at Osier, the halfway point. Travel in late September or early October to enjoy changing aspens. For information, call (800) 724-5451 or log on to www.cumbrestoltec.com.

KASHA–KATUWE TENT ROCKS NATIONAL MONUMENT
New Mexico's newest national monument protects 4,100 acres of eerie, minaret-shaped cones of pale volcanic tuff on lands sacred to Cochiti Pueblo. Managed by the BLM and the Pueblo of Cochiti, Kasha-Katuwe ("white cliffs" in the Keresan language) is in the Jemez Volcanic Field, halfway between Santa Fe and Albuquerque. Volcanic eruptions six to seven million years ago left behind pumice, ash, and tuff deposits over 1,000 feet thick as well as small, rounded, translucent obsidian fragments, dubbed "Apache Tears." The beige- and pink-striped tent formations are the result of differential erosion by wind and water, which also cut canyons and arroyos. The easy 1.2-mile Cave Loop Trail takes you through passageways in the Tent Rocks and is magical under snowfall. The steep, narrow, 1.5-mile Canyon Trail climbs 650 feet to a mesatop for panoramic views. For information, call (505) 761-8700 or log on to www.nm.blm.gov.

LINCOLN STATE MONUMENT

Tiny Lincoln, in southeastern New Mexico's ranchlands, was the scene of outlaw Billy the Kid's greatest escapades. When the Kid's employer, English rancher John Henry Tunstall was shot dead by members of a rival business ring on February 13, 1878, the Kid and Tunstall's business partner McSween sought to avenge his death. On April 1, 1878, the Kid shot and killed Sheriff Bill Brady, fled, and was captured, tried in Mesilla, and returned to Lincoln, where he was placed under house arrest at the house of Juan Patron, a merchant, and nearby Ellis Store. He then bust out of the Old Lincoln County Courthouse, only to be cornered and shot by Sheriff Pat Garrett in Pete Maxwell's farmhouse near Fort Sumner on July 14, 1881. Lincoln is now a national historical landmark, with over a dozen restored structures cooperatively run by the Museum of New Mexico and Historic Lincoln, a division of the Hubbard Museum of the American West in Ruidoso. Walking tour information is available at Lincoln State Monument in the Tunstall Store (575-653-4372) and Anderson-Freeman Visitors Center and Museum (575-653-4025). A three-day Last Escape of Billy the Kid Pageant is held every August. For information, log on to www.nmmonuments.org.

LIVING DESERT ZOO and GARDENS STATE PARK

This superb zoo in Carlsbad is the perfect place to learn about the 200,000-square-mile Chihuahuan Desert. A 1.3-mile natural trail passes through several habitats, from sand hills along the Pecos River to gypsum formations of the desert uplands and the pinyon-juniper zone of the hills. Living Desert cares for more than 200 species of animals that have been rescued and rehabilitated after injury in the wild. Look for black bear, bison, mountain lion, bobcat, and numerous birds, from roadrunners to eagles. Of particular interest are endangered Mexican wolves, part of a captive breeding program designed to reintroduce wolves into the Southwest. The gardens contain 300 plant species, including lechuguilla, sotol, agave, and other signature Chihuahuan plants. The four-day Apache Mescal Roast, the third weekend in May, includes arts and crafts, traditional dances, and a chance to taste mescal, the cooked heart of the agave, an Apache ceremonial food. For information, call (575) 887-5516 or log on to www.emnrd.state.nm.us.

MUSEUM of NEW MEXICO

The Museum of New Mexico is really five Santa Fe museums. The Museum of New Mexico History, located in the 400-year-old Palace of the Governors on the Plaza, traces New Mexico's history through exhibits of maps, documents, old photographs, and artifacts such as guns, spurs, pottery, period furniture, clothing, and a ceremonial death cart. The nearby New Mexico Museum of Art occupies a photogenic 1917 Pueblo Revival building and concentrates on 20th-century art by New Mexico artists like Georgia O'Keeffe, the so-called Cinco Pintores, as well as expatriate Taos artists like Dorothy Brett and Nicholai Fechin. The other museums are on Museum Hill, off Old Santa Fe Trail. The very popular Museum of International Folk Art houses the world's largest collection of international folk art displayed in fascinating dioramas; Spanish colonial folk art and textiles, costumes, and masks occupy separate wings. The Museum of Indian Arts and Culture displays some of the 70,000 prehistoric artifacts excavated by archaeologist Edgar Lee Hewett and others and stored in the adjoining Laboratory of Anthropology. Finally, the new Museum of Spanish Colonial Arts exhibits 3,000 artifacts collected by the

Cumbres & Toltec Scenic Railroad. PHOTO ©LAURENCE PARENT

Kasha–Katuwe Tent Rocks National Monument. PHOTO ©TERRY DONNELLY

Spanish Colonial Arts Society, which runs the annual Spanish Market. For information, call (575) 827-6451 or log on to www.museumofnewmexico.org.

Interior courtyard, New Mexico Museum of Art, Santa Fe. PHOTO ©LAURENCE PARENT

Ruts of the Santa Fe Trail at Fort Union National Monument. PHOTO ©GEORGE H.H. HUEY

ORILLA VERDE NATIONAL RECREATION AREA

New Mexico's most popular whitewater river run is located in the Rio Grande Gorge, south of Taos, where it has been dubbed "the Box" due to the narrowness of the dark volcanic canyon. Set aside as a state park in 1959, "the Box" itself was designated a Wild and Scenic River and transferred to federal management in 1970. The rest of the state park was transferred to the BLM and renamed Orilla Verde National Recreation Area. Access is from Pilar, a small Hispanic artist's community on NM 68 that was once home to Jicarilla Apaches. The Rio Grande Gorge Visitor Center, at the intersection of NM 570 and NM 68, is open daily and has information on river running, hiking, camping, and other recreation. Day trips on the river are operated by outfitters in Santa Fe and Taos. For information, call (575) 751-4899 or log on to www.nm.blm.org.

RIO GRANDE NATURE CENTER STATE PARK

This 270-acre preserve on the Rio Grande in Albuquerque has three ponds, nature trails, and outdoor classroom, a native herb and wildflower garden, and access to the Rio Grande Open Space corridor. A nice little visitor center blends well into the *bosque* bottomlands and has exhibits on Rio Grande water and porthole windows out to the main pond. The library viewing area is miked to the outdoors, so you can sit in here and listen to the enchanting sounds of red-winged blackbirds, geese, ducks, and other birds. Guided hikes and family activities are offered regularly. The park's rehabilitation center for injured birds is open occasionally. For information, call (575) 344-7240 or log on to www.emnrd.state.nm.us.

SALMON RUIN COUNTY PARK

This excellent small county park in Bloomfield preserves a 217-room Chaco-style great house pueblo built in A.D. 1088. Residents were corn specialists who grew a hardy form of corn in "waffle gardens," fields laid in a grid of water-conserving depressions. They probably traded it to Chaco Canyon along an extensive road system that passed through nearby Kurtz Canyon and the San Juan River via Aztec Pueblo to the north and Twin Angels Pueblo to the east. Salmon was abandoned in 1138, then reoccupied briefly in 1185 by Mesa Verdeans whose black-on-white pottery was found in great numbers when the ruins were excavated in the 1970s. A self-guided trail from the kiva-shaped visitor center descends to the ruins. Another trail takes you through the Salmon family homestead, where you can see a 19th-century adobe home, a Navajo hogan, a Ute brush wickiup, and a Jicarilla Apache tipi. For information, call (575) 632-2013.

SANTA FE NATIONAL HISTORIC TRAIL

Overseen by the National Park Service, this historic trail commemorates the 900-mile-long commercial trail that connected Missouri with Santa Fe between 1821 and 1880. American traders filled wagons with thousands of dollars worth of goods and headed west along the trail, fighting their way through blizzards, dust storms, grizzly bear attacks, and hostile Indian territory. Their reward for a successful trip was riches beyond measure and a taste of Santa Fe's free-living lifestyle of wine, women, dancing, and song. The U.S. Army of the West marched the trail to peacefully take New Mexico in 1846, and after 1848, traders also supplied U.S. Army forts built to protect the new U.S. citizens and travelers on the trail. The Santa Fe Trail was overshadowed by the arrival of the railroad in 1880. Fort Union National Monument and Pecos National Historical Park preserve trail ruts. They can also be seen in Kiowa Grasslands National Preserve, near Clayton. For information, call (505) 988-6888 or log on to www.nps.gov.safe.

SMOKEY BEAR HISTORICAL STATE PARK

The entire village of Capitan, in southeastern New Mexico, is dedicated to one furry creature: Smokey Bear, a real-life black bear cub who, on May 9, 1950, was rescued from a forest fire in the nearby Capitan Mountains. The whole family will enjoy the delightful Smokey Bear State Historical Park. There are exhibits on the history of the Smokey Bear fire prevention campaign, which predated the rescue of "Hotfoot Teddy," as Smokey was originally called. Another section looks at fire ecology in the West, the need for controlled burns, fire ethics, and the lives of "hotshot" firefighters, or "smoke jumpers," who risk their lives in the frontlines of a fire. Smokey Bear lived out the rest of his life at Washington National Zoo but is buried here along a pleasant nature trail. For information, call (505) 354-2748 or log on to www.emnrd.state.nm.us.

THREE RIVERS PETROGLYPH SITE

This BLM site in the northern end of the Tularosa Basin, about 41 miles from Alamogordo, preserves 21,000 petroglyphs carved by the mysterious Jornada Mogollon people a thousand years ago. A variety of extraordinary images, from handprints, sunbursts, and masks to birds and other cryptic symbols, decorate the lava rocks left behind by eruptions in the nearby Valley of Fires Recreation Area, west of Carrizozo. Sadly, vandalism has degraded many petroglyphs, although trained onsite stewards have now been hired by managers to watch over the site. A short trail leads through the site to a partially excavated pithouse and pueblo village. You can picnic and camp here but there is little shade and it's very hot in summer. For information, call (505) 525-4300 or log on to www.nm.blm.gov.

VALLES CALDERA NATIONAL PRESERVE

Throughout the 20th century, 89,000-acre Valles Caldera and parts of the surrounding Pajarito Plateau adjoining Bandelier National Monument were nominated for national park status. But because it was in private ownership as the Baca Ranch, powerful grazing and logging interests blocked federal efforts to purchase the property. It was finally set aside as a national preserve in 2000, when the federal government bough the ranch for $101 million. It is neither overseen by the park service nor the forest service but a completely new entity: a nine-member board of trustees appointed by the U.S. President, including ranchers, forestry experts, government officials, and environmentalists. The goal is to make the preserve completely self-sustaining by paying for all operational costs through grazing, timber sales, and public use fees. The current management plan is still being reviewed and adjusted. Currently, to visit the preserve, you must make a reservation in advance for a specific day and time and pay a use fee (averaging $20 - $25). Many activities are possible, including wildlife viewing (the preserve has an enormous herd of Roosevelt elk), long hikes into the caldera, horse-drawn wagon and sleigh rides, van tours, snowshoeing and cross-country skiing, elk hunting and fishing by lottery, and special events such as marathons, tracking workshops, and stargazing. For information and reservations call (877) 851-8946 or log on to www.vallescaldera.gov.

Great Kiva, Salmon Ruin County Park. PHOTO ©TOM DANIELSEN

Petroglyphs at Three Rivers Petroglyph Site. PHOTO ©EDUARDO FUSS

Valle Grande, Valles Caldera National Preserve. PHOTO ©LAURENCE PARENT

Adjoining National Parks

White House, Canyon de Chelly National Monument. PHOTO ©RANDY PRENTICE

CANYON de CHELLY NATIONAL MONUMENT

Canyon de Chelly is a 1,000-foot-deep canyon system carved into northeastern Arizona's Defiance Plateau by the Rio de Chelly. Navajos tend fields and livestock next to more than 700 ruined multistory cliff pueblos built by Kayenta Pueblo people between the 11th and 13th centuries. Peach trees planted by the Hopi, who are descended from the Ancestral Pueblo culture, still grow in the canyon. Canyon de Chelly has played a central role in Navajo history. In 1805, a long-running campaign by Spanish settlers led to the massacre of 115 Navajos in Massacre Cave. In 1849, the Navajo signed a peace treaty at the site of today's monument visitor center acknowledging United States rule, but by 1864, it had degenerated into war, subjugation, and between the years 1864–1868, incarceration of 9,000 Navajos in a concentration camp in eastern New Mexico. The surviving Navajo were allowed to return to their homeland in 1868, where a reservation was created for them by the U.S. government. Two scenic rim drives offer views of Antelope House, Mummy Cave ruin, Junction Ruin, and other pueblos as well as Navajo homesteads. Canyon entry is restricted to a steep 2.5-mile trail to White House Ruin. Navajo guides at the 1902 Thunderbird Lodge offer half- and full-day tours.

GRAND CANYON NATIONAL PARK

At northern Arizona's Grand Canyon, the 1,440-mile-long Colorado River has carved a 277-mile-long, mile-deep canyon, dropping 2,000 feet through a series of whitewater rapids between Lees Ferry and Grand Wash Cliffs to create one of the world's most astonishing chasms. The Colorado River averages 300 feet wide and 40 feet deep, but the actions of tributary streams, rain, ice, wind, and gravity have widened the canyon to an astonishing 18 miles and created a beautiful labyrinth of buttes, temples, and sheer cliffs. Most visitors arrive at the South Rim, via paved roads from Flagstaff and Williams. The historic Grand Canyon Railway, between Williams and Grand Canyon Village, makes a good day trip and cuts down on parking problems. The Santa Fe Railroad and concessionaire Fred Harvey built hotels, restaurants, stores, and galleries. Many are still operating today, including Bright Angel Lodge, Hopi House, Lookout Studio, Phantom Ranch, and Desert Watch Tower. They were designed by Mary Elizabeth Jane Colter, who was inspired by the Southwest's indigenous materials and cultures. Hikers and mule riders enter the canyon via the Bright Angel and South Kaibab trails and other steep, undeveloped trails blazed by miners. A bus system accesses the East and West Rim scenic drives. At 8,000 feet, the North Rim is higher and cooler. Access is via a 44-mile scenic highway from Jacob Lake, off US 89A. Rustic Grand Canyon Lodge and Cabins and the pleasant piney campground overlook Bright Angel Canyon; the main stem is visible from 23-mile Cape Royal Road. The North Rim is closed between October and May due to heavy snows.

GUADALUPE MOUNTAINS NATIONAL PARK

This north Texas park preserves the uplifted portion of the same Permian Reef found below ground in Carlsbad Caverns. Eighty miles of trails crisscross the Chihuahuan Desert and lead into the forested high country to 8,749-foot Guadalupe Peak, Texas's highest mountain. In fall (the best time to visit), changing Texas madrone, oak, and other deciduous trees along the year-round stream in McKittrick Canyon offer eye-popping color and many photo opportunities. On this trail, you can also visit the stone cabin built by oil geologist Wallace Pratt, who fell in love with the Guadalupes and, along with local rancher J. C. Hunter, helped establish the national park here in 1972. The Permian Reef Geology Trail offers a chance to examine the Permian Reef up close. Frijoles Ranch History Museum is open intermittently. A stop on the 19th-century cross-country mail route, the Butterfield Stage, can be seen near the park's pleasant primitive campground, which makes a good base for touring the area. Guadalupe Mountains National Park is 55 miles southwest of Carlsbad on US 62/180.

MESA VERDE NATIONAL PARK

Located in the Four Corners, off US 160 in southwest Colorado's Mancos Valley, Mesa Verde is an 80-square-mile park preserving 4,400 archaeological sites, including 600 cliff dwellings built by Ancestral Pueblo people between A.D. 550 and 1300 atop a green tableland: Mesa Verde. Excavated by archaeologist Richard Wetherill in 1888, the two most visited ruins—Cliff Palace and harder-to-reach Balcony House—sit on 12-mile Wetherill Mesa Road on Chapin Mesa and can only be visited by hour-long ranger-led tours in summer. Tickets are only available at Far View Visitor Center. To also visit Long House Ruin, on Wetherill Mesa, plan carefully: it's a 45-minute drive away. The park's second largest archaeological site is the easiest to access. Woodsy Spruce Tree House, behind Park Headquarters

Sunset from Mather Point, Grand Canyon National Park. PHOTO ©TOM DANIELSEN

Boulders beneath El Capitan, Guadalupe Mountains National Park. PHOTO ©WILLARD CLAY

The Mittens at sunrise, Monument Valley Navajo Tribal Park. PHOTO ©TIM FITZHARRIS

Cliff Palace at dusk, Mesa Verde National Park. PHOTO ©GEORGE H.H. HUEY

and the Chapin Archaeological Museum, is open year round and requires no ticket. Far View Lodge, the park's attractive motel, has panoramic views to the Navajo reservation and an above-average park restaurant serving Native-inspired food. Mesa Verde, the adjoining Ute Mountain Ute Reservation, Hovenweep National Monument, and BLM-managed Canyons of the Ancients National Monument are part of the longer Trail of the Ancients scenic byway. Information is available at the excellent Anasazi Heritage Center, 10 miles north of Cortez.

MONUMENT VALLEY NAVAJO TRIBAL PARK

Monument Valley isn't a valley at all but the Monument Upwarp, a geological uplift of strangely eroded De Chelly Sandstone and crumbly Organ Rock Shale stretching from Comb Ridge and the San Juan River in the north to Monument Valley and Black Mesa in the south. From the visitor center, a 17-mile dirt road leads to 11 spectacular vistas of the Mittens, Totem Pole, Full Moon Arch, and other formations made famous in John Ford Westerns like *Stagecoach*. Horseback, hiking, Jeep, and van tours emphasize Ancestral Pueblo culture and the contemporary traditional way of life of Navajo residents. They can be arranged (cash only) at the visitor center or Goulding's Lodge, the inn started in the 1930s by trader Harry Goulding and his wife "Mike." Gouldings has lodging, a restaurant, a campground, a gas station/convenience store with ATM, and a small museum. Monument Valley is located off US 163, 20 miles north of Kayenta. Navajo National Monument, 28 miles west of Kayenta, protects two of the best-preserved cliff dwellings in America and makes a good companion visit to Monument Valley.

RESOURCES & INFORMATION

NATIONAL PARKS

NATIONAL PARK SERVICE
SOUTHWEST REGION
P.O. Box 728
Santa Fe, NM 87504
(505) 988-6016
www.nps.gov

AZTEC RUINS
NATIONAL MONUMENT
84 County Road 2900
(Ruins Road)
Aztec, NM 87410
(505) 334-6174
www.nps.gov/azru

BANDELIER
NATIONAL MONUMENT
15 Entrance Road
Los Alamos, NM 87544
(505) 672-3861
www.nps.gov/band

CAPULIN VOLCANO
NATIONAL MONUMENT
PO Box 40
Capulin, NM 88414
(575) 278-2201
www.nps.gov/cavo

CARLSBAD CAVERNS
NATIONAL PARK
3225 National Parks Hwy.
Carlsbad, NM 88220
(575) 785-2232
www.nps.gov/cave

CHACO CULTURE
NAT'L HISTORICAL PARK
PO Box 220
Nageezi, NM 87037
(505) 786-7014
www.nps.gov/chcu

EL MALPAIS
NATIONAL MONUMENT
123 E. Roosevelt Avenue
Grants, NM 87020
(505) 285-4641
www.nps.gov/elma

EL MORRO NATIONAL MONUMENT
HC 61, Box 43
Ramah, NM 87321
(505) 783-4226
www.nps.gov/elmo

FORT UNION NATIONAL MONUMENT
PO Box 127
Watrous, NM 87753
(575) 425-8025
www.nps.gov/foun

GILA CLIFF DWELLINGS
NATIONAL MONUMENT
HC 68, Box 100
Silver City, NM 88061
(505) 536-9461
www.nps.gov/gicl

PECOS NATIONAL HISTORICAL PARK
PO Box 418
Pecos, NM 87552
(505) 757-6414
www.nps.gov/peco

PETROGLYPH NATIONAL MONUMENT
6001 Unser Blvd. NW
Albuquerque, NM 87120
(505) 899-0205
www.nps.gov/petr

SALINAS PUEBLO MISSIONS
NATIONAL MONUMENT
PO Box 517
Mountainair, NM 87036
(575) 847-2585
www.nps.gov/sapu

WHITE SANDS NATIONAL MONUMENT
PO Box 1086
Holloman, AFB, NM 88330
(505) 679-2599
www.nps.gov/whsa

NATIONAL TRAILS

EL CAMINO REAL DE
TIERRA ADENTRO
NAT'L HISTORIC TRAIL
www.nps.gov/elca
OLD SPANISH NATIONAL
HISTORIC TRAIL
www.nps.gov/olsp
SANTA FE NATIONAL
HISTORIC TRAIL
ww.nps.gov/safe
FOR INFORMATION
ON ALL TRAILS
National Trails System
PO Box 728
Santa Fe, NM 87504
(505) 988-6888

NATIONAL FORESTS

USDA FOREST SERVICE
SOUTHWEST
REGIONAL OFFICE
517 Gold Ave SW
Albuquerque, NM 87102
(505) 842-3292
www.fs.fed.us
CARSON NAT'L FOREST
208 Cruz Alta Road
Taos, NM 87571
(575) 758-6200
www.fs.fed.us/r3/carson/
CIBOLA NATIONAL FOREST
2113 Osuna Road NE, Suite A
Albuquerque, NM 87113
(505) 346-3900
www.fs.fed.us/r3/cibola/
GILA NATIONAL FOREST
3005 E. Camino del Bosque
Silver City, NM 88061
(575) 388-8201
www.fs.fed.us/r3/gils/
LINCOLN NATIONAL FOREST
1101 New York Avenue
Alamogordo, NM 88310
(575) 434-7200
www.fs.fed.us/r3/lincoln/

ABOVE: Chile ristras and Indian corn for sale in Taos. PHOTO ©KERRICK JAMES

SANTA FE NATIONAL FOREST

1474 Rodeo Road
Santa Fe, NM 87505
(505) 438-7840
www.fs.fed.us/r3/sfe/

GENERAL TRAVEL INFORMATION

ALBUQUERQUE CONVENTION AND VISITORS BUREAU

20 First Plaza, Suite 601
Albuquerque, NM 87102
(800) 284-2282
www.abqcvb.org

BUREAU OF LAND MANAGEMENT (BLM)

New Mexico Office
1474 Rodeo Rd
Santa Fe, NM 87502
(505) 438-7400
www.publiclands.org

GEORGIA O'KEEFFE MUSEUM

217 Johnson St.
Santa Fe, NM 87501
(505) 995-0785
www.okeeffemuseum.org

INDIAN PUEBLO CULTURAL CENTER

2401 12th St. NW
Albuquerque, NM
(505) 843-7270
www.indianpueblo.org

MUSEUM OF NEW MEXICO

105 E. Palace Ave
Santa Fe, NM 87501
(505) 827-6463
www.museumofnew-
mexico.org

NEW MEXICO PUBLIC LANDS INFORMATION CENTER—SANTA FE

1474 Rodeo Rd
Santa Fe, NM 87502
(505) 438-7542
www.publiclands.org

NEW MEXICO STATE PARK AND RECREATION DIVISION

408 Galisteo St.
Santa Fe, NM 87504
(505) 827-7173
www.emnrd.state.nm.us/nmparks

NEW MEXICO DEP'T OF TOURISM

491 Old Santa Fe Trail
Santa Fe, NM 87501
(505) 827-7400
www.newmexico.org

ROUTE 66 CORRIDOR PRESERVATION PROGRAM

P.O. Box 728
Santa Fe, NM 87504
(505) 988-6888
www.cr.nps.gov/rt66

SANTA FE CONVENTION AND VISITORS BUREAU

P.O. Box 909
Santa Fe, NM 87504
(505) 984-6760 or
(800) 777-2489
www.santafe.org

TAOS COUNTY CHAMBER OF COMMERCE

P.O. Drawer I
Taos, NM 87571
(505) 758-3873 or
(800) 732-8267

PUEBLOS AND RESERVATIONS

ACOMA PUEBLO

PO Box 309
Pueblo of Acoma, NM 87034
(505) 552-6604
www.skycity.com

COCHITI PUEBLO

PO Box 70
Cochiti Pueblo, NM 87072
(505) 465-2244

ISLETA PUEBLO

PO Box 1270
Isleta Pueblo, NM 87022
(505) 869-3111
www.isletapueblo.com

JEMEZ PUEBLO

PO Box 100
Jemez Pueblo, NM 87024
(505) 834-7359
www.jemezpueblo.org

JICARILLA APACHE NATION

PO Box 507
Dulce, NM 87528
(575) 759-3242
www.jicarillaonline.com

LAGUNA PUEBLO

PO Box 194
Laguna Pueblo, NM 87026
(505) 552-6654
www.lagunapueblo.org

MESCALERO APACHE RESERVATION

PO Box 227
Mescalero Apache
Reservation, NM 88340
(575) 671-4494

NAMBE PUEBLO

Route 1, Box 117-BB
Nambe Pueblo, NM 87747
(505) 455-2036

NAVAJO NATION

PO Box 663
Window Rock, AZ 86515
(520) 871-6647 or (928) 871-6436
www.discovernavajo.com

PICURIS PUEBLO

PO Box 127
Picuris Pueblo, NM 87533
(575) 587-2519

POJOAQUE PUEBLO

39 Camino del Rincon, Ste 6
Pojoaque Pueblo, NM 87506
(505) 455-2278
www.citiesofgold.com/pueblomain.html

ABOVE: A profusion of chiles. PHOTO ©EDUARDO FUSS

SAN FELIPE PUEBLO
PO Box 4339
San Felipe Pueblo, NM 87001
(505) 867-3381

SAN ILDEFONSO PUEBLO
Route 5, Box 315-A
San Ildefonso Pueblo, NM 87506
(505) 455-2273

SAN JUAN PUEBLO
PO Box 1099
San Juan Pueblo, NM 87566
(505) 852-4400
www.ohkay.com

SANDIA PUEBLO
Box 6008
Bernalillo, NM 87004
(505) 455-2278
www.sandiapueblo.nsn.us

SANTA ANA PUEBLO
2 Dove Road
Bernalillo, NM 87004
(505) 867-3301
www.santaana.org

SANTA CLARA PUEBLO
PO Box 580
Española, NM 87532
(505) 753-7330

SANTA DOMINGO PUEBLO
PO Box 99
Santa Domingo Pueblo, NM
87052
(505) 465-2214

TAOS PUEBLO
Taos, NM 87571
(575) 758-9593
www.taospueblo.com

TESEQUE PUEBLO
Route 42, Box 360-T
Santa Fe, NM 87506
(505) 983-2667

ZIA PUEBLO
135 Capitol Square Drive
Zia Pueblo, NM 87053
(505) 867-3304

ZUNI PUEBLO
Zuni, NM 87327
(505) 782-7238
www.ashiwi.org

FESTIVALS, FAIRS & ART MARKETS
JANUARY
PICURIS PUEBLO—
Kings Day Celebration Dance
NAMBE PUEBLO—
Buffalo, Deer, and Antelope Dances

SAN ILDEFONSO FEAST DAY—
Buffalo, Deer, and Comanche Dances
TAOS PUEBLO—
Turtle, Buffalo, or Deer Dances

FEBRUARY
PICURIS PUEBLO—

Candelaria Day Celebration Dances.
SAN JUAN PUEBLO—Deer Dances
MARCH
**RIO GRANDE
ARTS AND CRAFTS FESTIVAL—**
State Fairgrounds,
Albuquerque
ROCKHOUND ROUNDUP—
Southwest NM State
Fairgrounds, Deming
LAGUNA PUEBLO—
St. Joseph's Feast Day Harvest and dances.

APRIL
EASTER CELEBRATION DANCES—
At most pueblos
GATHERING OF NATIONS POWWOW—
University Arena, Albuquerque

MAY
CINCO DE MAYO—
Festivals held throughout
New Mexico to celebrate
liberation from French
occupation.
**JEMEZ RED ROCKS ARTS
AND CRAFTS FESTIVAL—**
Jemez Pueblo
SANTA CRUZ FEAST DAY—
Blessings of the Corn
and Field Dance, Taos Pueblo
SANTA MARIA FEAST DAY—
Dances at Acoma Pueblo
ST. PHILLIP'S FEAST DAY—
Dances at San Felipe Pueblo

JUNE
TESUQUE PUEBLO—Blessings
of the Field. Corn Dance.
SANTA ANA PUEBLO—
Corn Dances
**NEW MEXICO ARTS AND
CRAFTS FAIR—**
New Mexico State Fair-
grounds. Albuquerque.
RODEO DE SANTA FE—
Santa Fe Rodeo Grounds.
SANTA CLARA PUEBLO—
San Antonio Feast Day and
Comanche Dance.
**SAN JUAN PUEBLO
FEAST DAY—**
Buffalo, Corn, and Comanche
Dances.
SAN ILDEFONSO PUEBLO—
St. Anthony's Feast Day.
**SANTA FE TRAIL
RENDEZVOUS—**Raton.

JULY
**EIGHT NORTHERN INDIAN PUEBLOS
ARTS AND CRAFTS FAIR—**San Juan Pueblo.
**JICARILLA APACHE LITTLE BEAVER
ROUNDUP AND RODEO—**Dulce.
**MESCALERO APACHE CEREMONIAL
DANCES—**Dances, powwow, Indian food,
parade, and rodeo.Mescalero Apache
Reservation.
SANTO DOMINGO PUEBLO—

San Buenaventura Feast Day.

LAGUNA PUEBLO—
Santa Ana Feast Day.

SANTA FE INTERNATIONAL FOLK ART FESTIVAL—
Museum Hill. Worldwide folk artists converge on Milner Plaza for two-day event.

SANTA FE WINE FESTIVAL—
El Rancho de la Golondrinas.

TAOS PUEBLO—Santiago Feast Day Corn Dance.

TAOS PUEBLO—Powwow.

TRADITIONAL SPANISH MARKET—Santa Fe Plaza. Features the work of more than 300 artisans. Accompanied by a Contemporary Spanish Market nearby.

AUGUST

BAT FLIGHT BREAKFAST—
Outdoor breakfast at Carlsbad Caverns National Park as thousands of bats return to breed in the caverns.

INTERTRIBAL INDIAN CEREMONIAL—A huge powwow at Red Rock State Park, Gallup. Arts and crafts, parades, rodeo, and food.

OLD LINCOLN DAYS—
Billy the Kid, etc. in Lincoln.

ACOMA PUEBLO—
San Lorenzo Feast Day

COCHITI PUEBLO—
San Lorenzo Feast Day

SANTA CLARA PUEBLO—
Santa Clara Feast Day. Buffalo, Harvest, or Corn Dance.

SANTA FE INDIAN MARKET—
Santa Fe Plaza. The largest in the world. Book hotels well in advance.

SANTO DOMINGO PUEBLO—
Santo Domingo Pueblo Feast Day. Corn Dance.

ZUNI TRIBAL FAIR—Zuni Pueblo.

SEPTEMBER

ANNUAL NAVAJO NATION FAIR—
Red Rock State Park, Gallup. Rodeo, carnival, parades, intertribal powwow, Miss Navajo Nation Pageant, food, concerts.

SAN JUAN PUEBLO—Harvest Dances.

HATCH CHILE FESTIVAL—
Celebrates the chile harvest. Hatch.

INTERNATIONAL BAT FESTIVAL—
Carlsbad Caverns National Park.

NEW MEXICO STATE FAIR—
One of the largest fairs in the nation, with PRCA rodeo and western recording artists.

State Fairgrounds, Albuquerque.

NEW MEXICO WINE FESTIVAL—Bernalillo.

ACOMA PUEBLO—
San Estevan Feast Day and Harvest Dance.

TAOS PUEBLO—
San Geronimo Feast Day. Sunset dance, foot race, pole climbing, social dances, trade fair.

JICARILLA APACHE RESERVATION—
Stone Lake Fiesta

TAOS FALL ARTS FESTIVAL—
Concerts, gallery openings, dances, etc.

TAOS TRADE FAIR—
Costumed interpreters bring the Spanish colonial and mountain man period to life at La Hacienda de los Martinez.

OCTOBER

ALBUQUERQUE INTERNATIONAL BALLOON FIESTA—
World's largest gathering of hot-air balloons over a nine–day festival. Balloon Fiesta Park.

LINCOLN COUNTY COWBOY SYMPOSIUM—
Ruidoso Downs.

NORTHERN NAVAJO NATION FAIR—
Shiprock Fairgrounds.

SOUTHERN NEW MEXICO STATE FAIR—
Dona Ana County Fairgrounds. Las Cruces.

NOVEMBER

FESTIVAL OF THE CRANES—
Celebrating the return of thousands of sandhill and whooping cranes, snow geese, etc. to wetlands along Rio Grande. Bosque del Apache NWR. Socorro.

TESUQUE PUEBLO—San Diego Feast Day Buffalo, Corn, Comanche, and Deer Dances.

DECEMBER

CANYON ROAD FAROLITO WALK—
Brown-bag lanterns (farolitos) and small fires (luminarias) light Canyon Road during annual stroll. Musicians, food, drink, and carol singing.

CHRISTMAS CELEBRATIONS—
Acoma, San Ildefonso, Tesuque, Santa Clara, Nambe, Laguna, San Juan, Taos, Zia, and Picuris Pueblos. Call for details.

WINTER SPANISH MARKET—
Winter version of popular summer market. Location TBD.

PRODUCTION CREDITS

Publisher: Jeff D. Nicholas
Author: Nicky Leach
Consulting Editor: Chris Judson
Illustrations: Darlece Cleveland
Printing Coordination: Sung In Printing America

ISBN 13: 978-1-58071-074-9
ISBN 10: 1-58071-074-3
©2008 Panorama International Productions, Inc.

SIERRA PRESS
4988 Gold Leaf Drive, Mariposa, CA 95338
(209) 966-5071, 966-5073 (Fax)

Visit our Website:
www.NationalParksUSA.com

OPPOSITE
The walls of Abó, Salinas Pueblo Mission National Monument. PHOTO ©MICHAEL COLLIER
BELOW
Exotic erosional patterns, Bisti Badlands.
PHOTO ©CARR CLIFTON